The Corridors of Time ·V·

THE STEPPE & THE SOWN

By HAROLD PEAKE and
HERBERT JOHN FLEURE

NEW HAVEN · YALE UNIVERSITY PRESS
LONDON · HUMPHREY MILFORD
OXFORD UNIVERSITY PRESS
1928

445-95-

PREFACE

FROM time immemorial the peaceful grain-growers, fully engaged with the cultivation of their crops, have suffered from the depredations of nomad pastoral folk, who wandered with their flocks and herds on the waste spaces around them. Such raids have been of constant recurrence throughout the history of the Old World, in the Far East with greater frequency and until more recent times than in the West. Such raids have repeatedly destroyed civilizations for a time, though the conquerors have usually become civilized by their subjects. Thus a new civilization has arisen, rejuvenated by the fresh air of the steppes and deserts.

This volume deals with the first of such raids that took place on a large scale, destroying as it did the Old Kingdom in Egypt, and bringing to an end by a more gradual process the rule of the city states of Sumer. That raids, all of great magnitude, should have occurred almost simultaneously in many parts of the Near East, has led some writers to believe that the whole series were occasioned by a period of prolonged drought, leading to a diminished grass supply in the steppes and deserts. This may be so, but we have pointed out another, either additional or alternative, cause : the taming of the horse.

Many thanks are due to the authors, editors, and publishers of the following works and journals for permission to reproduce figures : *Pflanzen- und Tierverbreitung*, 1899, by A. Kirchhoff (F. Tempsky, Vienna), for fig. 2; 'La Pontide préscythique', in *Eurasia Septentrionalis Antiqua*, vol. i, by A. M. Tallgren (La Société Finlandaise d'Archéologie), for figs. 6, 8, 9, 12, 13, and 14 ; *Iranians and Greeks in South Russia*, by M. Rostovtzeff (Clarendon Press), for fig. 7 ; *Dawn of European Civilization*, by V. Gordon Childe (Kegan Paul, Trench, Trubner & Co., Ltd.), for figs. 9, 44, 46, and 70; *Salaminia*, by A. P. di Cesnola (Kegan Paul, Trench, Trubner & Co., Ltd.), for fig. 64*a* ; *British Museum Quarterly*,

Preface   3

vol. ii, no. 2, for fig. 11*d* ; *Reallexikon der Vorgeschichte*, vols. vi, vii, and viii (Walter du Gruyter, Berlin), for figs. 21, 31, and 67 ; *Prehistoric Thessaly*, by A. J. B. Wace and M. S. Thompson (Cambridge University Press), for figs. 23–5 and 63*b* ; *Studies in Early Pottery of the Near East*, Part II, by H. Frankfort (Royal Anthropological Institute), for figs. 27, 32, 63*a*, and 64*c* ; *Primeval Man in Central Europe*, by P. Goessler (Franckh'sche Verlagshandlung, Stuttgart), for figs. 28–30 ; *Fonds de Cabanes néolithiques du Nirva et de Bassenge*, by Marcel de Puydt (Societé d'Anthropologie de Bruxelles), for fig. 33; *The Lake Dwellings of Switzerland and Other Parts of Europe*, 1866, by F. Keller (Longmans, Green & Co., Ltd.), for figs. 36, 37, 40, and 41 ; *Human Origins*, by G. G. MacCurdy (D. Appleton & Company, New York), for fig. 43 ; *Explorations in the Island of Mochlos*, by R. B. Seager (American School of Classical Studies at Athens), for figs. 48, 55–7, 59, and 62 ; *Troy*, by W. Leaf (Macmillan & Co., Ltd.), for fig. 50 ; *Les civilisations préhelléniques de la mer Égée*, by René Dussaud (Librairie Paul Geuthner, Paris), for fig. 51; *Ilios*, by H. Schliemann (John Murray), for figs. 52, 53*a*, 63*c*, and 64*b* ; *Südwesteuropäische Megalithkultur*, by Wilke (Curt Kabitzsch, Würzburg), for fig. 65 ; *Manuel d'archéologie préhistorique celtique et gallo-romaine*, vol. ii, by J. Déchelette (Librairie Alphonse Picard et fils, Paris), for figs. 66 and 74 ; *Mém. de l'Acad. des Sci. et Lettres de Montpellier*, for fig. 71 ; *The Stone and Bronze Ages in Italy*, by T. E. Peet (Clarendon Press), for fig. 73 ; *Découvertes en Chaldée*, by E. de Sarzec (Librairie Ernest Leroux, Paris), for fig. 76.

H. J. E. P.
H. J. F.

August 1928.

CONTENTS

1. Life on the Steppes 7
2. The Northern Steppes 20
3. The Dispersal from the Steppe 38
4. New Arrivals in Greece 52
5. The Spread of the Peasants 59
6. The Lake-dwellers of Central Europe 69
7. Maritime Activity in the Aegean 82
8. The Second City of Hissarlik 91
9. Crete 99
10. Maritime Trade 109
11. The Last Days of Sumer 128
12. Chaos in Egypt 139
13. Chronological Summary 145

Index 158

LIST OF ILLUSTRATIONS

1. The Sahara Desert. Photograph by E. N. A. 9
2. The South Russian Steppe 11
3. Map of the Northern Steppe 13
4. Model of a covered wagon from a Wei tomb. From a photograph of a specimen in the Royal Ontario Museum, Toronto, by the courtesy of Professor C. T. Curelly 17
5. A lamasery in Mongolia. Photograph by courtesy of Mr. L. H. Dudley Buxton 18
6. Earthenware figurines from the kurgan of Oul, Kuban . . . 22
7. Plan of the grave at Maikop 23
8. The Tzarevskaya cists 25
9. Basket-like and ovoid pots from Jackowice 27
10. The Ulski tent. Photograph by courtesy of Dr. G. Boroffka . . 29
11. Metal battle-axes from Tzarevskaya, Maikop, and Ur. The last reproduced by the courtesy of the Trustees of the British Museum . 30
12. Stone battle-axes from South Russia. After A. M. Tallgren . . 31
13. Hammer-headed pins 33
14. Catacomb grave 35

15. Copper axes from Cemetery A at Kish. After E. MacKay, *Report on
the Excavation of the ' A ' Cemetery at Kish, Mesopotamia*, Part I,
by courtesy of the Field Museum of Natural History, Chicago . 37
16. Figure of a mounted man from Kish. Photograph by courtesy of
Professor S. Langdon 39
17. Map of Turkestan, Persia, and North-West India 41
18. Pottery from Mohenjo-daro. Photograph by courtesy of Sir John
Marshall, C.I.E., Litt.D., Director-General of Archaeology in India 42
19. Map of China showing the distribution of early painted pottery . 43
20. Painted pottery from China 45
21. Pottery of the Second Danubian period from Lengyel and Jordansmühl 47
22. Map showing the distribution of the Fatyanovo culture . . 49
23. Plan of Dhimini. After Tsountas 53
24. Megara at Dhimini. After Tsountas 54
25. Bowl from Dhimini. After Tsountas 55
26. Map of Thessaly and adjoining regions 56
27. Fragments of ware, believed to be Danubian, from Tiryns. Photograph by courtesy of Dr. H. Frankfort 57
28. Vases from Hinkelstein 60
29. Pottery of the Rössen type 61
30. Pottery from Flomborn 63
31. Münchshofen ware 64
32. Pottery from Butmir. Photograph by courtesy of Dr. H. Frankfort 65
33. Omalian pottery from La Hesbaye 66
34. Map showing the Spread of the Peasants 67
35. Early Neolithic pottery from Port-Conty 71
36. Horn objects from Moosseedorf 73
37. Stacked platform from Lake Niederwyl (Egelsee) 75
38. Reconstruction of Neolithic Pile-dwellings at Unter-Uhldingen on
Lake Constance, after R. R. Schmidt. Photograph by Dr.
Douglas Guthrie 76
39. Three types of ' sleeves ' from Vinelz. Photograph by courtesy of
M. O. Tschumi 77
40. Two shoulderless sleeves from Meilen 78
41. Perforated stag-antler hammers from Meilen 79
42. Map of Central Europe showing the distribution of lake-dwellings . 81
43. Large pieces of beeswax flint from Grand Pressigny. After Henri
Martin 81
44. Cycladic sherd and ' frying-pan ' depicting boats 83
45. Plan of a house in the First City of Phylakopi. After T. D. Atkinson 84
46. Tomb group from Amorgos 85
47. Clay tablet from Boghaz Keui in the Halys basin. British Museum 87
48. Pottery of the Third Early Cycladic period 89
49. The site of Troy to-day 92
50. The south gate of Hissarlik II. Third period 93
51. Battle-axe from Treasure L, No. 1 of Hissarlik II . . . 95
52. Vases from Hissarlik II 96
53. Face-decorated wares from Hissarlik II and Cemetery A at Kish.
Photograph of the latter by courtesy of Field Museum of Natural
History, Chicago 97

54. Map of Crete 100
55. Pottery of the Second Early Minoan period 101
56. Stone bowl from Mochlos 102
57. Gold objects from Mochlos 103
58. Flat axes, cutters, and forceps from Mochlos. After R. B. Seager . 104
59. Double axe from Mochlos 105
60. Triangular and long daggers from Mochlos. After R. B. Seager . 106
61. Plans of chamber tombs of Nos. I, II, and III at Mochlos. After
     R. B. Seager 107
62. Saucer of Syrian type 108
63. High-handled cups from Sicily (Photograph by courtesy of Dr. H.
     Frankfort), Thessaly, and Hissarlik 111
64. Schnabelkannen from Cyprus, Hissarlik, Cyclades (Photograph by
     courtesy of Dr. H. Frankfort), and Sardinia. After Pinza, *Mon.
     Ant.*) 113
65. Multiple vases from France, Spain, Hissarlik, Italy, and Egypt . 114
66. The Treasury of Atreus at Mycenae 115
67. Tombs in the island of Leukas 117
68. Rock-cut tomb in Sicily. After Pinza, *Mon. Ant.* . . . 119
69. Figurines of fat women from Hal Saflieni, Malta. By courtesy of
     Dr. Charles Singer and the Royal Anthropological Institute . 120
70. Megalithic tomb at Anghelu Ruju 121
71. The Grotte-des-Fées, near Arles 122
72. Map of the trade-routes in the Mediterranean 123
73. Fragments of incised ware from Matera 125
74. Knobbed bone objects from Hissarlik and Sicily 126
75. Seated figure of Gudea. Photograph, Giraudon 131
76. Copper figures of bulls surmounting cones which were employed as
     votive offerings in the reigns of Gudea and Dungi . . . 132
77. Map of Mesopotamia and the surrounding regions . . . 135
78. Chronological chart of kings of Mesopotamia 137
79. Statue of Mere, a Theban prince. British Museum . . . 143
80. Map showing the distribution of Danubian civilization about 2500 B.C. 149
81. Map showing the distribution of Danubian civilization about 2400 B.C. 151
82. Map showing the distribution of Danubian civilization about 2300 B.C. 153
83. Map showing the distribution of Danubian civilization about 2200 B.C. 155
84. Chronological Chart . . . . *end-paper*

I

Life on the Steppes

THE term grass-lands suggests great open treeless spaces with herds of animals and groups of nomad men, and we are too apt to think of them as all very much alike. We may have no difficulty in realizing that the grass-lands within the tropics are distinct from the rest in respect of the plants, animals, and men to be found there; but those outside the tropics are all labelled steppes, and it becomes necessary for our purpose to emphasize the contrasts between the northern and southern groups of these steppes in the northern hemisphere of the Old World. They approach one another, but remain divided by the line of the Elburz range and the Hindu Kush. To the south lie the grass-lands of Western India, Baluchistan, Afghanistan, Persia, Arabia, and North Africa; to the north they stretch between Hungary on the west and the Sea of Okhotsk on the north-east.

The above-mentioned southern grass-lands were far wetter than now in the early days of modern man; but, with the northward shift of climatic belts (*Hunters and Artists*, p. 97), large areas became desert, and what remained of the steppe was but a dry fringe of the riverine areas. The change of climate led to pressure of population near the rivers, and their more or less regular floods led men both to measure time and to take advantage of the fertilizing silt for the purpose of cultivating cereals. We have already suggested the association of this activity with numerous inventions (*Peasants and Potters*, ch. 2), and would now add that the idea of the city grew as part of the same scheme. The people of the southern steppe have thus worked out their fate in fairly frequent contact with irrigating cultivators, living in the world's earliest cities. They have developed activities complementary to those of the tillers, herding instead of cultivating, fighting rather than digging. The earliest domestic animals in the southern steppe were probably the ass and the goat, with sheep and cattle as very early intruders if not fully established from the outset. The one-humped camel seems to be native to Arabia and reached Egypt during the Old Kingdom; it was known there as early as the First Dynasty. Its domestication doubtless stimulated intercourse and so promoted trade, but it may have waited long before men bred it for its speed and usefulness in war, and it does not seem to have caused such a crisis as did the incoming of the horse. The latter, man's companion in war and his aid in the government of subjects and the management of herds, may be credited with being an important factor in the general overturning of ancient institutions and modes of life about the middle of the third millennium B.C. Ellsworth Huntington believes that this was also a time of severe droughts, and, if his views establish themselves, we have here an additional factor of unrest. It was clearly a period more disadvantageous to the cultivator than to the steppe-man, ever ready to move on or to fight. Of this we have echoes in the Book of Genesis, which emphasizes the feeling of superiority among the herders, the 'Sons of God'; the story also illustrates for us their relations with the sons and daughters of men in the cities near by.

The horse, however, could not become so important on the southern steppe lands as he became on those of the north. He is able to stand great cold and can paw the snow in search of food; he needs to feed very frequently on tenderer grasses than suffice for the ass and camel; and he requires a good deal to drink. He belongs essentially to the northern steppe, but he became a great ally of various rulers in southern steppe lands, notably of the Persian Kings of Kings, who had the cradle of their domain in the hill-region of Fars, a land where water and grass

Fig. 1. The Sahara Desert.

would keep the horses healthy. It seems to have been only late in history, perhaps even after the days of the Roman Empire, that the famous breed of Arab horses, inured to abstinence from food and drink, was evolved in Nejd, the central oasis of Arabia.

The southern steppe-life is better developed in Arabia and parts of Persia than in the Sahara, both because the land is higher and less sun-baked, and because these regions are near the ancient trade-routes that were naturally established between Sumer and Egypt. Among these nomad herdsmen, for whom discipline is very important, society is built on a basis of kinship; the lonely man has no place, and the kin has responsibility for its members. Several facts are associated with this. The first is the rule of the patriarch; the second, the regular succession of authority from father to son; the third, the practice of polygamy, which enabled the group to become larger and thus more powerful, and also to add to the number of routine labourers. The loneliness of the steppe has helped to develop a remarkable law of hospitality, so well described by Doughty, but this has not made the true steppe-man anxious to intermarry his sons with the daughters of the cultivators, the contrast of whose mode of living made Rebecca weary of her life (Genesis xxvii. 46). Such wives would hanker after the settled homes of the cities and be little apt for the hard work of pitching and striking the tents. Accordingly we find the herdsmen very proud of their genealogies, which seem to initiate history, and to have become ornamented with memories of long-past heroes, memories out of which grew the legends and heroic tales that beguile the immense leisure of the lonely steppe. Organized, disciplined, and mobile, the southern steppe-man has been apt for war, the more so because of his training through blood-feuds between different kin. He has often raided the cultivator, or exacted tribute from him for some form of protection that could easily grow into domination and enslavement, and he has needed to get grain from the cultivator as a supplement to his own food produce of milk and flesh, with the addition of dates gathered here and there. The mare cannot be used for milk on the southern steppe, and other milk is less complete and less suffi-

FIG. 2. The South Russian Steppe.

cient as a food; the northern steppe-man with his milch-mares offers a contrast in this respect, as we shall see.

The southern steppe-man has had manifold relations with the cities of the river-sides. He has dominated them from time to time, founding dynasties that have organized the cultivators. He has used the learned men of the city to write down the much-prized genealogies, as well as the epic narratives of the rulers' achievements, which these were now too much occupied with business to keep fully in mind. He has sought to combine his tribal customs of ritual observance and blood-feuds with the laws of the cultivator relating to the management and transfer of land. He has traded goods—gold, frankincense, and myrrh, slaves and spices—from town to town across the waste. He has learned the religious ideas of the people he has met, and again and again has endeavoured to combine them into that of a supreme God whom he regards initially as the father of his tribe. Thus the divine parentage of the patriarch, and especially of the steppe-man who has become king over cultivators, is a great feature of early history. These religious ideas have given birth in the course of time to Judaism and Islam, the two religions that have brought monotheism to its fullest development, and in both the veneration of the written word finds its completest expression. Thus have the towns and the wastes combined to give the southern steppe-man a unique place and influence in the story of civilization. We must now proceed to think of the northern steppes.

The northern steppe-lands present, and presented still more in the far past, conditions widely contrasted in different regions, and appear always to have shown contrasts with, as well as resemblances to, the southern steppe. The Sayan, Altai, Tian-shan, Pamir, and Hindu-Kush ranges, each lying more or less east and west, form a series of high curved lines stretching south-westward from Lake Baikal to the gate between the Hindu-Kush and the Elburz in Northern Persia. To the north and west of these ranges the land, while high around and especially to the east of Lake Baikal, is predominantly low from the east end of the Lena basin in north-east Asia right away to the lower Danube basin in south-east Europe. Only comparatively small areas rise above the 1,500 foot level and vast stretches have an altitude of less than 600 feet. To the south and east of the ranges, on the other hand, are plateaux generally well above the 1,500 foot level, with immense areas more than 3,000 feet above the sea. Tibet, south of these plateaux, is again distinct from them, since it stands in large measure at a height exceeding 15,000 feet. Between the Altai and Tian-shan ranges the low-land stretches some distance eastwards, and this gateway between the high plateaux and the more westerly lowland is known as Dzungaria.

Recent work has demonstrated that, when there were great

Fig. 3. Map of the Northern Steppe.

ice sheets in North-west Europe, the highlands of Central Asia, Tibet, and the plateaux were also glaciated. We may thence argue that, when the ice sheets reached their last great maximum during the Würm glaciation, the northern steppe-lands as a whole were almost, if not quite, uninhabitable by men of modern type. The ice sheet of North-west Europe, with its covering of dense cold air, shouldered the westerly winds and cyclones farther south than the zone they usually occupy at present; these cyclones, therefore, spread along the Mediterranean, and may have got into Asia across the Black and Caspian Seas, giving very heavy snow-falls on some of the mountain ranges named, as well as to some extent on the high plateaux. When the belts of climate moved northward again, the westerly winds and cyclones reached the Baltic rather than the Mediterranean, north instead of south of the belt of high atmospheric pressure which now so often stretches in winter from the Ural Mountains, past the high altitudes of Central Europe, to Spain. Consequently the supply of winter rain and snow in the great northern steppe, even in its lowland portion, was much reduced. Transcaspia, however, doubtless remained moist for a long time owing to the melting of the mountain ice. Spring moisture and a low rainfall thus became a feature of much of the lowland part of the northern steppe-lands, which have become more like deserts in recent millennia as the supply of water from the mountain ice has diminished. Conditions on the Mongolian plateaux must long have remained very forbidding, and still more so in Tibet.

The grass-lands became inhabited by flocks and herds of horses, camels, sheep, goats, and asses; cattle occupied the moister regions, the river-sides and the park-lands verging towards the northern forest, which, at first of pine and later of deciduous trees, fringed the steppe on that side. The borders of the northern steppe-lands 'towards the rain', whether in South Russia or in the far east along the feeders of the Hoangho, had acquired their characteristic loess soil, of fine-grained wind-blown material with a flavouring of organic matter from plants, during interglacial and late glacial phases, through the outblowing of the winds from the ice sheets over the loose detritus dropped by the melting ice edges. This soil has played an immense part in the subsequent life of the regions concerned.

Whether they first entered the northern steppe-lands along

the loess belt from Western Europe or through the gate between the Elburz and the Hindu-Kush, men of modern type came, and apparently trusted themselves, in the end, to the great sea of grass, following the herds and after a while exercising increasing control over them. We can imagine them driving a herd into a valley and penning it in at night with watch-fires; then, little by little, accustoming the beasts to their presence and ultimately to their control. The taming of the horse for war, and of milch-mares as a source of an exceptionally complete food, must have marked an immense advance, giving the herdsman a power over great spaces and enabling him to organize vast stretches to gratify his ambitions and to meet his needs.

Like his fellow in the southern steppe, the northern steppeman bases society on kinship and carries on the blood-feud; he, too, exercises a great hospitality, and keeps his pride of birth, his genealogies, and his heroic epics. He is ever ready to move or to fight; his material possessions, apart from his flocks and herds, are kept down to a minimum, and thus in many ways the life on the northern and southern steppes is akin. There are, however, marked contrasts to set against these similarities.

While some amount of cultivation was done, even in very early times, in Turkestan and in other northern regions, city life is not nearly so ancient nor so widespread in the northern steppe as it is in the southern, and trade, while not altogether absent, has here been very much less important. The steppe-man in the north has, therefore, had much less contact with cultivators, and his use of writing has been less extensive; so also his trading propensities and attendant exchanges of ideas have developed far less. Still, the men of the steppe borders, like those farther south, have repeatedly dominated neighbouring cultivators, usually village-dwellers, and have founded principalities that have profited from their power of command and of organization over large spaces.

Like their southern fellows, the northern steppe-folk have become expert tent-builders, though the shapes of the tents have been different. The long rectangular tent of black hide and the round tent of camel's hair are features of the southern steppe. In the northern tents are rectangular or round, but are said to be smaller than those of the southern lands. One type has a framework of bent branches, forming arches, the other is the gabled fly-tent with its framework of straight sticks, perhaps associated with the use of pines. In parts of the northern steppe near the forest borders the herds include especially large numbers of cattle, which cannot feed on the snow-covered steppe in winter as they lack the equine art of pawing away the snow. On the frozen marshes, however, near the rivers they would find long grass standing out through the snow as well as shoots of willow that are welcome food. It appears that steppe-folk must often have camped for the winter near streams, especially in the vicinity of park-lands, and would have built wattle-and-daub huts on the model of the tent. The park-lands offer shelter and rich pasture as the snow disappears and calving time comes round, and in these border lands of the steppe, both east and west, the wheeled ox-cart is an old-established feature; this has led Myres to distinguish wheeled nomads from the purer horse nomads. In many cases the ox-cart has a tent-like covering and has served not only as a conveyance but also as a habitation. Herodotus tells us that in his day some of the Scythians still lived in wagons; these the poet Aeschylus describes as 'lofty houses of wicker-work, on well-wheeled chariots'. The Wei Tartars, who made themselves masters of the northern part of the Chinese Empire in the third century of our era, seem to have lived in similarly covered wagons; models of these have been found in the tombs of these people.

Ellsworth Huntington in a series of books has stated and amended a theory of cycles of moisture and drought in Inner

Asia, each succeeding cycle being drier than its predecessor. This view has been disputed by Berg and others, who, however, agree that there was a change of climate at the end of the Ice Age. Stein has advanced the view that there was another change at a period not very remote from the beginning of the Christian era, when the supplies of water from past accumulations of

Fig. 4. Model of a covered wagon from a Wei tomb.

mountain ice greatly diminished. There seems to be a probability that the drying has been somewhat intermittent, even if the pulsation has been much less regular than Huntington supposes; that the desert has increased within the last 2,500 years is beyond all question.

Changes of climate have thus been important factors in the life of the northern as well as of the southern steppe, but the acquisition of command over the horse has been another factor that has caused steppe-men to spread into surrounding lands and to shake old civilizations to their foundations. On the high plateaux of Central Asia the terrible severity of winter seems to have led people in many cases to gather into closer quarters for the winters, and Huc tells us of their clustering round stoves fed by argols of dung and sleeping for long periods. Had we the space it would be interesting to follow out the relation of this habit to the spread and maintenance of the monastic establish-

Fig. 5. A lamasery in Mongolia.

ments or lamaseries, which are such a feature of the more fertile patches of the great highland region of Central Asia.

The loess regions east and west of the steppe have fertile soil not unduly encumbered with forest, and in both directions steppe-folk have spread as conquerors and organizers, with tremendous effect. Dominating the cultivators and apparently introducing the ox-plough, they have contributed to the spread and enhanced development of the habit of food production, and the combination of steppe-folk and cultivators gave birth in the third millennium B.C. to the germs of what has become the Chinese civilization, which has radiated out from the Weiho

Valley at the eastern end of Kansu. The influence of the northern steppe-folk in Europe will be discussed in later chapters. These formidable people have also spread south, and we shall discuss their influence in the middle of the third millennium B. C. upon Mesopotamia and more indirectly upon Egypt. They seem further to have moved into Seistan, and probably thence into India at a rather later date, giving rise to the Kshatriyas or horsed warriors, who still form the military caste in that land. The Persians of the kingdom of Cyrus and Darius seem to have been another group of northern steppe-folk, horsemen born.

The great spread from the northern steppe-lands in the third millennium took the horse and the art of food production by means of the plough in many directions, and is thus a dominant factor of the history of civilization. The cult of the horse, often sacrificially eaten, the cult of the sun, and the idea of patriarchal primogeniture, are all associated with these movements. We do not know whether the driving power was the acquisition of complete control of the horse, or the spur of drought; quite probably both operated together, but the power of the steppe-folk echoes through the world's history, however little history they may have had in their own lands of solitude.

BOOKS

Huc, E. R. *Travels in Tartary, Thibet and China*, 1844–6 (London, 1852).
Huntington, Ellsworth. *The Pulse of Asia* (Boston, 1907).
Rostovtzeff, M. *The Iranians and Greeks in South Russia* (Oxford, 1922).
Doughty, C. M. *Travels in Arabia Deserta*. New Edition (London, 1923).
Childe, V. Gordon. *The Aryans* (London, 1926).

2

The Northern Steppes

IN this chapter and the next we shall endeavour to survey the evidence regarding South Russia in early times. We believe that this evidence tends to show that the steppe lands of South-east Russia were then inhabited by a people, who had developed a nomad pastoral civilization, as well as a more or less settled type of life in the park-lands on the northern fringe of the steppe. These people buried their dead in mounds, known as kurgans, where the bones are found covered with red ochre; they used as their distinctive weapon a perforated axe-hammer of stone, derived, as we believe, ultimately from Mesopotamia. We think that these men were evolving towards the Nordic race type that we have described in chapter 9 of *Peasants and Potters*, and that they may have been the creators of the Indo-European or Aryan group of languages.

The steppes of South Russia are dotted over with large mounds that are known locally as kurgans. Though some of these may be the remains of village sites, as are those at Anau in Turkestan, the majority are known to be barrows or burial mounds. A large number date from a relatively late time and contain remains that are believed to be those of the Scythians, but others have quite different contents and are known to be of a much earlier date, though how early is still uncertain. Others again may belong only to the Middle Ages, for some of the inhabitants of South Russia continued the practice of erecting them until then.

In the early type of kurgan are found skeletons of tall men, buried in a contracted position, the bones covered with red ochre. These, which are now known as the ochre-graves, are found scattered widely over South Russia, and even beyond, on

the Rumanian plain; they are, however, confined to the grass-
lands, or at the most only just penetrate the park-lands to the
north. Their distribution, as Childe has pointed out, coincides
in this region with that of microlithic flints of epipalaeolithic
times ; the distributions of both agree with that of the grass-
lands. Hitherto they have not been found east of the Volga,
and Childe has assumed that this was their eastern boundary.
On the other hand, with the exception of those at Anau, few
of the kurgans of Turkestan have been explored, and as the
Volga would have presented no serious obstacle and the grass-
lands extend throughout Turkestan, it seems probable that the
people responsible for these ochre-graves roamed over much of
the region lying between the Carpathians and the Hindu-Kush,
though parts of it may have been too wet.

The kurgans in the basins of the Don and Donetz have been
divided into three successive groups by Ebert. The oldest
graves were pits, lined with rough stone walling, each containing
one contracted skeleton and surmounted by a kurgan. In most
of these there was no metal, or very few and humble articles of
copper; the pots, few in number, were simple ovoid beakers,
decorated with impressions of cords, sometimes in the form
of inverted triangles. In the second period the skeletons had
been placed in what have been called catacomb graves, closely
resembling the pit-caves that have been found in Euboea;
these, too, were surmounted by a kurgan. In these catacomb
graves sixty-six per cent. of the implements were of metal,
usually if not invariably of copper, but the forms were simple.
Stone mace-heads, either spherical or pear-shaped, were used at
this time, silver rings, copper beads, some of which seem to have
been derived from the Cyclades, and even glass beads were used
as ornaments. Female figurines in earthenware have also been
found in these tombs. The pots were flat-bottomed, ornamented
with a decoration of loops and spirals. The kurgans of the third

period belong for the most part to the iron age and may be considered as Scythic or, at least, as influenced by Scythic culture.

Unfortunately the kurgans in other parts of the steppe have not been studied with equal thoroughness and we cannot be

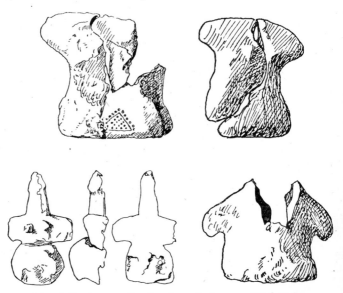

FIG. 6. Earthenware figurines from the kurgan of Oul, Kuban.

sure of the successive stages of culture. The catacomb graves have not been reported from other parts and it is dangerous to argue from the proportion of metal implements, since the graves near the Caucasus are always rich in metal while those to the north-west contain little or none. From this it has been argued that the north-western graves are the older, but our experience in the Danube basin, as discussed in the preceding volume of this series, has shown us that it is dangerous to argue that lack of metal necessarily betokens an earlier date. The Caucasus lies much nearer to Mesopotamia and other centres of civilization than do the north-western graves, so its

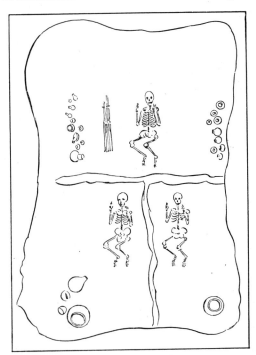

Fig. 7. Plan of the grave at Maikop.

people had better opportunities of learning the art of metallurgy and so of supplying themselves with such luxuries as metal weapons and ornaments.

The most famous kurgan in this rich neighbourhood is that cleared away in 1897 and 1898 from the centre of the town of Maikop, which lies in the basin of the Kuban River at the northern foot of the Caucasus range. Here was a great shaft-grave, lined with wood and divided into two compartments. In one of these a warrior had been buried under a canopy supported by posts with golden finials in the forms of bulls and lions. The grave contained three bodies; these were adorned with beads, rings, and other jewels, and accompanied by metal flasks and a stone bowl with a neck and lid of gold. In spite of this evidence of wealth and the elaborate workmanship of the jewellery, the forms of the bowls and flasks were primitive. Amongst other objects found in the grave were a copper battle-axe of Meso-potamian type, a two-bladed axe-adze, and two types of flint implements that suggest Tardenoisian forms.

Higher up the same valley, near Tzarevskaya, a different type of tomb was found containing red-ochred skeletons; these had been interred in two cists of upright stones. Each of these was a long cist divided into two compartments by an upright slab; these slabs were pierced, in one case with a square and in the other with a circular hole. Such stone cists, which are not un-like the wooden chambers at Maikop, but built of well-squared megalithic blocks, have been found in considerable numbers in the upper part of the Kuban Valley, and along the coast of the Black Sea westward to the Crimea ; they occur also in the Caucasus. Excepting those near Tzarevskaya, they have always been found rifled of their contents. The circular hole, or port-hole as it has been called, is a usual feature, and occurs else-where. The extent and the interpretation of its distribution will be discussed in the next volume.

The contents of the Tzarevskaya cists, though much poorer than those of the graves at Maikop, resemble them to some extent, though the gold and silver pots are here replaced by pots of earthenware. These are globular with incised decoration around the neck and on the shoulders. Flat celts, perforated battle-axes, knife daggers, a tanged spear-head, and other objects of pure copper, lay with the skeletons, as well as rings of silver, gold, and copper wire, and beads of carnelian and gold. Besides these there were many arrow-heads and lance-heads of finely flaked flint. In spite of their relative poverty, these tombs cannot be separated by any great distance of time from those at Maikop, and from the fact that an older grave of the shaft type had been disturbed when they were made, we must conclude that neither these nor those of Maikop belonged to the first period. On the other hand, the primitive forms of the pots

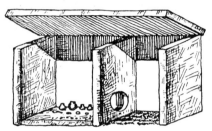

Fig. 8. The Tzarevskaya cists.

and weapons, and the fact that the latter were of copper and not of bronze, preclude us from placing them in the third period.

The date of the Maikop tombs has been hotly disputed, and there is no general agreement on the question. Both Tallgren and Rostovtzeff have drawn attention to a certain resemblance between the jewellery at Maikop and that found in the Second City at Hissarlik, though bronze was known before the latter city was destroyed, while copper only is found at Maikop. If we accept this view, we shall not be far wrong in placing Ebert's second period as approximately contemporary with the second settlement at Hissarlik, which in a later chapter we shall date between 2600 and 1900 B.C., and in relegating the simple shaft graves of his first period to centuries earlier than this. On one point, however, we must be on our guard. In the valley of the

Kuban and in the Donetz region the changes which usher in the second period seem to be due to influences from the Aegean, or perhaps from South-west Asia, the connexions between which and the Aegean are well known. Such influences become negligible as we proceed north and west. Here, therefore, the simple shaft graves may have remained in use until a much later date.

As we have seen, the contents of the graves become poorer and the proportion of metal objects smaller as we pass north and west. This is well seen from the description of the grave at Jackowice, near Kiev, where spiral tubes of copper and earrings of the same form with flattened ends were the only metal objects found. The pots were of the ovoid type common in the Don-Donetz region, and there were curious basket-shaped vessels, which occur also in Kherson, just north of the Crimea. In the group of kurgans at Jackowice were some which contained skeletons not reddened with ochre, and we may suspect that here, on the very edge of the steppe, the people who used red ochre met and mixed with others who were skilled in basketry. These basket-like pots may remind us of those, based on a leather prototype, which the early Danubians had made after mixing with the Epipalaeolithic people on their border.

Akin to the people of the Russian grass-lands were others living in the park-lands to the north, and, if we may judge from the Jackowice pottery, the latter had mixed to some extent with basket-making people in an Epipalaeolithic stage of culture. It seems probable that the potter's art, once introduced to these Epipalaeolithic hunters, spread to the west and north-west, for at a later date we shall meet with a ware, known as string-ornamented ware or cord pottery, that seems to have been derived ultimately from the pottery of the Russian steppe.

Following Spitsyn, Childe has well summed up the main cultural characteristics of these early peoples of the Russian steppe, the ochre-grave folk; 'In addition to flint chips and stone hammer-axes the most notable weapons are flat copper spear-heads and stone mace-heads. As ornaments, besides bored teeth, spiral ear-rings with flattened ends of silver or copper, and hammer-headed pins of bone or copper were worn. Silver is unusually common, but amber was found only once in a barrow in Chernigov.'

The people seem to have been fairly tall and long-headed, with a proportion of extremely long and high heads. Unfortunately the data for individuals from graves of different

FIG. 9. Basket-like and ovoid pots from Jackowice.

periods are not clearly distinguished in most of the descriptions that are available.

Bones of sheep and horses have been found in the ochre graves, especially east of the Dnieper. This seems to indicate that, in this region at least, the graves belonged to a pastoral people. It is true that grain has been found in some of their kurgans, and it has been thought that some of them may have practised agriculture; on the other hand they may have obtained this by barter or forcible seizure from some neighbouring settled folk. Childe is of opinion that they moved about in tilt wagons, and cites, in support of this, a clay model found at Ulski on the Kuban. This was found low down in a kurgan,

and above it was a grave containing an extended skeleton
with some gold and copper beads and two alabaster statuettes
resembling early Cycladic types. The line drawing of this
object certainly suggests a wagon, but two photographs of it,
which we reproduce, and which were sent to us very kindly
by M. G. Boroffka, the Keeper of the Scythian Antiquities
at the Hermitage Museum at Leningrad, are not nearly so
convincing. M. Boroffka tells us that in Russia it is thought that
this model represents a tent. It appears to us that it is either
the model of a tent, made gipsy-fashion with long bent willow
poles, or else a hut of wattle and daub constructed on the model
of such a tent.

Copper battle-axes and copper gouges, resembling those found
in the kurgans of the Kuban region, have been found here and
there on the South Russian plain. As one passes northwards and
westwards they diminish in number and their place is taken by
perforated stone battle-axes of a very similar type. Childe,
quite rightly as we believe, considers these battle-axes, whether
of copper or stone, and pottery ornamented with impressions
of twisted cords, as the essential features of the culture of these
ochre-grave folk.

The origin of these battle-axes is much disputed. Childe was
the first to point out their close resemblance to perforated axes
from Mesopotamia, and some of those from Maikop are almost
if not quite identical with some early examples from that
district. The view put forward by Kossinna is that the copper
axes were derived from the stone battle-axes, which become
more common as we reach the Baltic, and that they would thus
ultimately be derived from the perforated axes or hammers of
bone used by the folk at Maglemose in Denmark, whose culture
we described in our second volume. We believe that there are
serious difficulties in accepting the latter hypothesis. Some of
the Maikop axes are almost identical in form with those from

Fig. 10. The Ulski tent.

Mesopotamia; on the other hand, no transitional types have been found leading gradually from the Maglemose axes to the stone battle-axes. The earliest battle-axes from Denmark seem to be those found in the 'single-graves' of Jutland, and these can

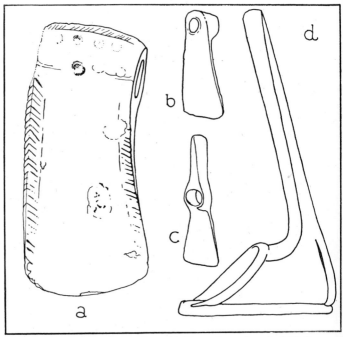

Fig. 11. Metal battle-axes from (a) Tzarevskaya, (b and c) Maikop, and (d) Ur.

hardly be earlier than, if as early as, 2200 B.C. We have seen reason for thinking that the early shaft graves of the ochre-grave folk, at any rate east of the Dnieper, are probably earlier than 2600 B.C. The general opinion in Scandinavia and Britain is that the single-grave people of Jutland were immigrants from the south-east and brought with them the stone battle-axe and fine pottery, including a form which is known as the beaker and which will be discussed in the next volume.

To meet this difficulty Tallgren has recently argued for a much later date for the ochre graves. He has pointed out that a razor at Maikop resembles one from a tomb of the M.M. III period at Mochlos and therefore dates between 1700 and 1600 B.C.; that a poker-butted spear-head from Tzarevskaya

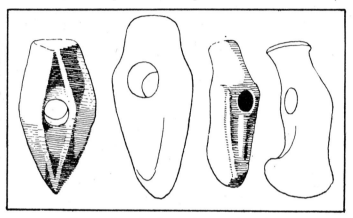

Fig. 12. Stone Battle-axes from South Russia.

resembles one from a Hittite grave at Carchemish, dating from between 1900 and 1750 B.C., while a dagger with a bronze hilt from the same site resembles some from Bohemia which are dated between 1750 and 1450 B.C. On the other hand, a segmented bone bead from a catacomb grave at Novogrigoryevka on the Dnieper resembles some in stone from Vrokastro, of the E.M. II period, dating, therefore, from 2800 to 2400 B.C., while a copper disk from the same grave resembles one from Stollhof in Austria, which is dated at 1800 B.C., and hammer-headed pins from this grave resemble some found at much later sites in Greece. These later Greek pins are probably survivals from earlier periods, and the kurgans quoted may date from any time between 2800 and 1600 B.C. They all belong, however, to the second stage of South Russian steppe culture which we think began at or perhaps before 2600 B.C. This period may well have lasted 1,000 years, and the culture in question, which is far from uniform, may have remained in use until 1600 B.C. or even later. Some winged beads from Konstantinovka near Novocherkask, which resemble beads of the E.M. III period from Paros, date from between 2400 and 2100 B.C., while some copper ear-rings from Jackowice near Kiev, have parallels from the Second City of Hissarlik, which will be described in a later chapter.

We believe, therefore, that the second period of the ochre graves may be considered as having lasted approximately from 2600 to 1600 B.C. or later, and the first period preceded 2600 B.C., though how early it began it is impossible as yet to surmise. The custom of covering the corpse with red ochre before burial goes back to an early phase of the Upper Palaeolithic Age, and the habits and utensils of nomad pastoral folk are very persistent.

The facts, admittedly few and far from complete, can best, in our opinion, be explained by supposing that many of the late Palaeolithic hunters left Western Europe as the forest spread, and followed their game back to the Russo-Turkestan Steppe. As the change of climate continued their numbers were reinforced by the arrival, in late Tardenoisian times, of descendants of the Final Capsian invaders of Spain, or of other hunting folk who had learned to use their weapons. These hunted cattle in the park-lands, sheep on the mountains to the south, and horses on the grass-lands. Ultimately they domesticated the two former animals and finally the horse, which, as we believe, was the last to be tamed, and may have been subdued only a short time before the period with which we are now dealing. About 2600 B.C., or conceivably a little earlier, traders, perhaps from the Cyclades, but perhaps from some port on the coast of Asia Minor, had

come into contact with some of these nomads at the mouths of
the Kuban and the Don, and had provided the Kuban people
with weapons of metal and ornaments of copper and silver, to

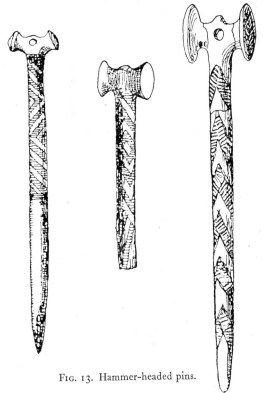

FIG. 13. Hammer-headed pins.

supplement the goods which they had obtained by trading with,
or more probably raiding, the people dwelling to the south of
the Caucasus; they had also introduced to the dwellers by the
Don the type of tomb known as the catacomb grave, as well as

weapons and beads of metal. The dates that we have adopted seem forced on us by a number of factors, widely spread around the steppe, which would be inexplicable were later dates adopted. These factors we shall describe in the next chapters.

This chapter must not close without a word on the language problems connected with the early peoples of South Russia. During the greater part of the nineteenth century a considerable section of the learned world was engaged in studying the origins and history of the languages of Europe. They discovered that nearly all the European tongues were allied, and, together with certain languages of Asia, formed a well-defined group. Of these the most primitive seemed to be Sanskrit, the ancient speech of the Hindus and one parent of the more important languages of India. As the speakers of these tongues distinguished themselves from others as Aryas, the group of languages was at first called Aryan. Later it was pointed out that this term belonged more appropriately to the Indian languages of the group together with ancient Persian and a few other allied dialects, and the term Indo-Germanic came into use in Central Europe. The prominence of the second half of this term did not please those living in Western Europe, so the term Indo-European was substituted. This has been felt by many to be an unwieldy term, so Dr. Peter Giles has recently suggested that the name of Wiros be applied to those who use or have used these tongues, but this term, though short and convenient, has met with little favour either in this country or elsewhere.

The earlier students of language were intent on discovering where these languages originated or on determining what they called the Aryan cradle. As Sanskrit appeared the most primitive of the Indo-European tongues, they looked to Asia for the source of the group, and most of them favoured the western slopes of the Hindu Kush. One only, Dr. Latham, advocated a European cradle, but his opinions were ridiculed on the Continent. By degrees it was discovered that Old Lithuanian, spoken on the south-east shores of the Baltic, was quite as primitive as Sanskrit, and opinion changed towards a European origin. Many suggestions were made in turn, which it is unnecessary to enumerate here, for these views have been dealt with elsewhere by one of the present authors. But towards the close of the nineteenth century, before any general agreement

FIG. 14. Catacomb grave.

had been achieved, such studies were abandoned in this country, and, in spite of continued work in Central Europe, the question of the Aryan cradle relapsed into obscurity.

Recently Childe has restated the problem for English readers, and, bringing to bear on it all the recently acquired knowledge of prehistoric archaeology and physical anthropology, has argued that the grass-lands of Russia, in which he does not include Turkestan, were part, at least, of the Aryan cradle. Kossinna, on the other hand, believes that the ochre-grave folk migrated to South Russia from the Baltic, and is inclined to think of the Baltic as a part, at least, of the Aryan cradle, and, if Tallgren's dates for South Russian beginnings were to be accepted, there might be a good deal to be said for this view.

Rostovtzeff, however, dated the beginnings of South Russian civilization far back in the third millennium, and we have seen it is highly probable that a Mesopotamian copper axe is the prototype of the metal and stone axes with shaft holes used in South Russia. The cultural connexions between Mesopotamia and South Russia are fairly numerous, and must date far back in the third millennium. As to the route connecting them little can as yet be said, but the recent discovery by Hrozný of what seems to have been a long-established mercantile depot at Kara Euyuk, containing objects dating from the latter part of the third millennium, hints that the connexion may have been through Anatolia.

Reference has been made to the figurines or idols in the early graves in South Russia, and to their obvious relationship to similar figures in early graves in the Cyclades. Whether this represents a link between the Cyclades and South Russia or a connexion between both and some part of Asia Minor must remain uncertain until more is known from Asiatic sites. If the Mesopotamian origin of South Russian civilization be admitted, it seems inevitable that we should think of the spread of the battle-axe, copied in stone from a metal model, from South Russia to the Baltic.

The battle-axe seems to have reached this goal during the period of the passage graves, and the idea of a spread of civilization to the Baltic from the south-east helps to interpret the finds of that region, to which the use of metal spread relatively late.

Anthropological researches on modern populations in Sweden and in Norway suggest that the people of these lands include survivors of late Palaeolithic types, and it is probable that migrants from South Russia to the Baltic in the third millennium would meet Epipalaeolithic folk on their way, and may have had these elements among them from the start.

We have seen that Childe has produced evidence for his belief that some early people of South Russia spoke a primitive Indo-European tongue, which they carried to most of those parts of Europe and Asia in which it or its derivatives have subsequently been spoken. We should be inclined, for the reasons we have stated, to consider the grass-land of South Russia and Turkestan

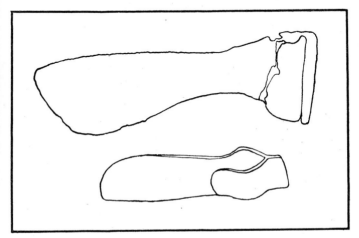

Fig. 15. Copper axes from Cemetery A at Kish.

together as the area in which these tongues developed, and from which they spread.

To add to our picture we may say that the Kuban area offers an environment of special interest. In climate it differs somewhat from the steppe, and it enjoys the benefit of maritime influences from the Black Sea. It has its river and is able to grow fruit. It is thus a small 'region of increment' in close proximity to both steppe and sea, as well as to the mountains of the Caucasus. In such a region of the steppe border may well have occurred an intermingling of steppe-nomads and settled folk doing some amount of cultivation, as soon as that art had spread from South-west Asia, where we believe that it originated. The character of the richer graves, such as that at Maikop, suggests the craftsmanship of settled people, while, as already explained, some features hint also at a nomadic tradition. We should, therefore, be inclined to suggest that in the Kuban valley is one of the numerous settled areas in which steppe-nomads and cultivators united. As to language we would further suggest that steppe-nomads, making many contacts with cultivators, would probably develop a language adapted to spread, a language with fewer inflexions and with less complicated sounds than would be characteristic of those spoken by groups of peasants or forest-dwellers. It seems to us that the hypothesis of conquering horse-nomads of the steppe-borders, spreading in time across Europe north-westwards to the Baltic, best interprets the facts at present at our disposal.

BOOKS

CHILDE, V. GORDON. *The Dawn of European Civilization* (London, 1925).
CHILDE, V. GORDON. *The Aryans* (London, 1926).
ROSTOVTZEFF, M. *Iranians and Greeks in South Russia* (Oxford, 1922).
MINNS, ELLIS H. *Scythians and Greeks* (Cambridge, 1913).
PEAKE, HAROLD. *The Bronze Age and the Celtic World* (London, 1922).

3
The Dispersal from the Steppe

IN our preceding volume, when describing the fortunes of the kings of Agade, we had occasion to mention difficulties that arose during the closing years of the reign of Sargon, about 2700 B.C. About that time he carried out a successful expedition against unruly tribes dwelling to the north of his kingdom between the Tigris and the Euphrates, but their raids began again under every succeeding monarch, and one suspects that it was their constant attacks which ultimately brought the dynasty of Agade to an end.

The country occupied by these people was known to the people of Agade as Sub-artu, and to the Sumerian people of Ur as Sua-ki, Su-ki or Su. The name of the people seems to have been Su or Subir. It is clear from names and words that have come down to us that the language of these people was neither

Fig. 16. Figure of a mounted man from Kish.

Semitic nor Sumerian, and it is thought that it had affinities with the tongue of the Mitannians, who afterwards occupied this territory, and with one of the dialects of the Hittites, who were established a little later in Asia Minor. Now there is evidence that both these latter languages had certain Indo-European affinities, which can best be interpreted by supposing that the rulers were of Indo-European speech. This, as we have seen, seems to have been the speech of the Northern Steppe-folk. The inference is that the people of Su, and a neighbouring folk usually associated with them, the people of Gu, were, as far as their rulers were concerned, of this Indo-European stock from the Northern Steppe. If this were so, some of these Northern Steppe-folk had left their steppe and penetrated southwards into the north of Mesopotamia by 2700 B.C.

Whether the people of Su and Gu were horsemen we have no evidence. It is commonly believed that the horse was introduced into Mesopotamia by the Kassites, another people thought to be Indo-European, nearly a thousand years later. This animal is, however, found mentioned in a tablet of the time of Hammurabi, between 2067 and 2034 B.C., where it is called the ass from the east. It has been claimed that it was known in Mesopotamia still earlier. In 1925 Langdon excavated a palace at Kish, which he believes was abandoned at the time of the foundation of Agade, just before 2700 B.C. On the site of the palace he found a cemetery, and in one of the tombs a clay model, which he believes to be that of a horse and its rider. Langdon claimed that these tombs dated from a time prior to the abandonment of the palace, but this is by no means proved. If, however, his contention is correct, the figure of the horse and rider cannot be later than the very beginning of the reign of Sargon, and so may well represent a mounted warrior from Sub-artu. On the other hand, it may well be that the figure represents a man riding an ass.

We have seen that at a date which we have fixed provisionally at about 2600 B.C., though it may well have been a century or two earlier, the settlement at Anau in Turkestan came to an end. Pumpelly, who excavated the site, believed that the abandonment of the village was due to drought. He thought that the streams, rising in the mountains to the south, by which their crops had been irrigated, had ceased to flow, and that the inhabitants had been compelled to move to a more favourable situation. This may be so, but, since we shall find that the Northern Steppe-folk were at this time raiding other settled communities, it is possible that the abandonment of the North

Kurgan at Anau was due to their attacks. These may also have been due to the drought, though another cause may have been a recently increased mastery of the horse.

Whatever the cause may have been that led to the abandonment of the village of Anau, there seems to have been about this time a great dispersal of people who, like the inhabitants of that

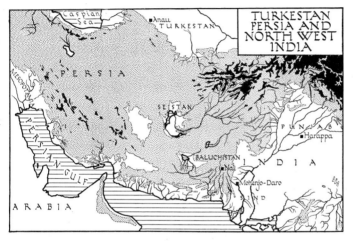

FIG. 17.

village, made and used painted pottery. Sherds of painted pottery have been found by Sir Aurel Stein in Seistan to the south, others have been found farther to the east at Nal in Baluchistan, while pottery that seems to be of the same type has recently been unearthed by Sir John Marshall at Mohenjo-daro in Sind and at Harappa in the Punjab, on sites that Hall believes date from before 2500 B.C.

Again, similar pottery has been found still farther east by Dr. J. G. Andersson of the Chinese Geological Survey. Sites containing pottery of this type and a few copper objects have been discovered in the valley of the Si-ning, a tributary of the Hoang-Ho, and at Chen-Fan, on the southern edge of the Gobi Desert, both in the province of Kansu. Other sites still farther east

FIG. 18. Pottery from Mohenjo-daro. Photograph by courtesy of Sir John Marshall, C.I.E., Litt.D., Director-General of Archaeology in India.

have yielded a greater abundance of potsherds but no metal. Those so far reported are at Yang Shao Tsun and Pu Chao Chai, in the district of Mien Chih Hsien, and at Ching Wang Chai and Chih Kai Chai, in the district of the Yin Hsien, all in the province of Honan. Other remains of the same kind have been

found in the cave of the Sha Kuo T'un, in the Chin Hsi district
of the province of Feng-tien in Southern Manchuria.

The date of these Chinese settlements is uncertain, but it
is agreed that they are very early. According to the traditions
embodied in the Shu King, one of the sacred books of the Chinese,
the empire was founded by Yao in the year 2357 B. C. Many sino-

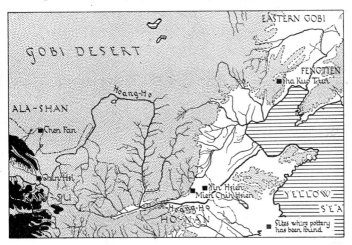

FIG. 19. Map of China showing the distribution of early painted pottery.

logists are not prepared to accept as historical the earlier portions
of this narrative, and Hirth declines to accept any date earlier
than 776 B. C., while the native historian, Sema Ts'ien, who wrote
about A. D. 180, begins his history at 841 B. C. In some quarters,
however, there has been a disposition recently to attach greater
value to the narrative of the Shu King, though all admit that
one document has been interpolated at a later date. Von
Richtofen, a generation ago, held that the Shu King was a valu-
able source of information.

It is agreed by all that civilization reached China from the west, down the Wei Valley. The empire of Yao had its centre in that valley near its junction with the Hoang-Ho. The sites in Kansu, where the painted pottery and copper were found, are connected with the upper reaches of the Wei Valley by an easy pass, so it is not impossible that these settlements date from between 2500 and 2400 B.C. Dr. Arne would place them 500 years earlier, since tradition attributes the introduction of agriculture to Shen Nung (2739–2705 B.C.).

On the west we have more certain evidence. At a date that cannot be very far from 2600 B.C. the first settlement at Cucu-teni, on the Moldavian Plain, which we have described in the preceding volume, was destroyed, though it was rebuilt again soon afterwards. Erösd, too, the early settlement in Transyl-vania, was destroyed about the same time and was not refounded. Doubtless these two settlements were not the only victims, but no other villages of this period have yet been explored in this region, except one at Usatov, near Odessa, and no detailed account of this has yet reached this country. The early villages in the Tripolje district, near Kiev, were also destroyed about the same time. At Khalepji, in this region, a settlement had been destroyed and the materials used to erect a barrow for a man of the nomad race, who was buried in it, in a contracted position, with a single pot and his bones coloured with red ochre.

This ochre grave gives one a hint as to who were the de-stroyers of these settlements, and some sherds of cord orna-mented pottery, lying about above the debris at Erösd, seem to prove conclusively that the invaders were Steppe-folk pressing westward.

In the Danube basin we find at this time a marked change in the civilization. The old agricultural life continued as before, but new elements had been introduced from without. The shoe-last celts had grown in size, so as to resemble, in some cases,

FIG. 20. Painted pottery from China.

plough-shares. Pointed-butted axes of jadeite and other hard stones came into use as well as flint, and copper was more widely used, sometimes for axe-adzes and axe-hammers as on the Russian steppe. We find at this time cemeteries in which the dead are laid in the grave in a contracted position, the skeletons are those of tall, long-headed men, and sometimes by the side of the corpse had been placed a lump of red ochre. These features, taken together, can leave us in no doubt that the new elements of culture introduced at this time into the Danube basin were brought in by the Nordic Aryan-speaking people of the Russian steppe, who had destroyed the settlements of Cucuteni and Erösd.

The pottery changed gradually. The ware was black as before, but the habit of decorating it with incised ornament ceased, except at Vinča, where the incisions were filled in with white paste. The ware was henceforth decorated with bosses and spirals, moulded and applied to the surface, sometimes, too, by thick paint added before the wares had been polished and fired. This is called encrusted ware, and seems to be a poor imitation of the painted pottery of Erösd; it spread throughout the Danube basin as far as Moravia.

Though many of the old shapes survived, new forms came in, some introduced from Erösd, and others apparently from Hissarlik, with which there seems to have been considerable trade. This trade has been traced by Gordon Childe, who has cited imports from Hissarlik, or imitations of these products, that have been found in graves and settlements of this period along the courses of the Tisza and the Danube, and even still farther north in Silesia and Thuringia. It would seem from what he tells us that the people of Hissarlik were at this time exploiting the gold mines of Transylvania and the copper mines that occur in that country and in Eastern Hungary; it is even possible that they had discovered the tin deposits in Bohemia

FIG. 21. Pottery of the Second Danubian period from Lengyel, (c, f, g, h) and Jordansmühl (a, b, d, e).

and were importing that metal to make bronze. This question will, however, be discussed more fully in a later chapter.

In Moravia some of the people, perhaps the descendants of the Epipalaeolithic hunters, painted themselves red by means of clay stamps; beads and pendants of marble were introduced, as well as shell buttons with V perforations. Thus the arrival of the Steppe-folk made considerable changes in the life of the Danubian peasants, and probably developed their organization and increased their contacts with their neighbours.

There seems reason for believing that some of the Steppe-folk, or perhaps people of the park-lands to the north, spread about this time into Galicia and even as far west as Silesia; on the other hand, it is possible that the people in these parts, who used stone battle-axes, were descendants of the Epipalaeolithic inhabitants of the North European Plain, and had received these weapons and the potter's art from their neighbours in the park-lands.

Farther north, in the forest lands of Central Russia, in the Volga basin, we find at this time, or perhaps a little later, a culture known as that of Fatyanovo from the site at which it was first discovered. This civilization has elements that relate it to more than one culture. Some features connect it with the Epipalaeolithic culture of Finland and North Russia, others are thought to have arrived, but at a later date, from Jutland, while the hemispherical pots found on these sites clearly originated on the steppe. It may be said that this civilization arose from the mingling of several peoples some centuries later than the period that we are discussing, but it is possible that the element that came from the steppe may belong to the series of movements of which we have been treating in this chapter.

Whether, therefore, we look to India or to China or to Europe, we find indications of connexions with the ancient culture of Mesopotamia, and also evidence of disturbance and development

● Fatianovo culture sites ◉ Fatianovo itself ■ Sites at which some objects resembling those of Fatianovo culture have been found. V·M·L = Volga mixed lands

FIG. 22. Map showing the distribution of the Fatyanovo culture.

some time, perhaps some centuries, before the middle of the
third millennium B.C. Later we shall see some reason for thinking that during this phase of disturbance, not only did the
Second City of Hissarlik grow, but the Early Minoan cultures
of Crete developed, showing links with both the old Kingdom
of Egypt and the Asiatic shores, and, probably through the
latter, with Mesopotamia. As we shall see in a later chapter,
the fall of the old Kingdom in Egypt was rather later than the
disturbance of the old Mesopotamian civilization; it may well
have been a part of the series of troubles we have sketched here,
though delayed owing to the distance between the Nile valley
and the centre of disturbance.

Huntington thinks that the centuries following the middle
of the third millennium were a period of severe drought. We
have hinted above at the possibility that command of the horse
may have been an element in the power of outsiders, probably
steppe-people, to disturb the settled life of the old centres on
the Euphrates. The wealth of the folk on the South Russian
steppes about this time was the theme of our last chapter, and
an increase of drought, or an increase in the mobility of the
steppe-men, or both together, would inevitably disturb the
settled folk on their borders. If it is reasonable to suppose that
the flow of civilization to India and to China was part of this
disturbance, it is interesting to gather that the idea of cities
spread in this direction, to India at least and it may be to China
as well. Both on the Indus and along the Wei-Ho it was possible
to cultivate and irrigate and to renew the fertility of the soil,
in the one case from flood alluvium, in the other from fresh
loess near at hand. The renewal of fertility of the soil was, as
yet, a far more difficult problem in Europe, and in this direction
the idea of cities was not diffused to anything like the same
extent as in India.

Our view, then, is that people from the South Russian steppe, armed with axe-hammers, spread during this period into North-west Europe, which was then sprinkled with survivals of Epi-palaeolithic culture. There is much evidence, too, of an exten-sion of culture, including polished stone axes, southwards to the Sudan and beyond, at some period before the history of that region begins; we are inclined to consider this, again, as part of the same series of movements, but the horse appears not to have got into Africa at that time, not even into Egypt.

In fact we seem to be faced with one of the great crises of the world's history, with a spread of many arts around the peri-phery of the ancient civilizations, and with evidence of a new mobility that we associate with the increased use of the horse. That these contacts and movements should have disturbed seriously the ancient centres in Mesopotamia and Egypt seems only natural when we realize that wherever the complete mastery of the horse may have been achieved, it was certainly not in those regions. Thus we do not so much think of the Kuban, South-east Europe, India, China, and other regions as influenced by refugees from the ancient centres; rather do we picture a widespread activity with increased mobility and communication, combined with discipline. We think that these circumstances were well adapted to the rise and diffusion from the steppe borders of a language, or of a group of related forms of speech, and that their haphazard complexities were somewhat simplified by the contact with other peoples that followed these widespread movements, and by the use of these tongues of the conquerors by their subject peoples.

BOOKS

HUNTINGTON, ELLSWORTH. *The Pulse of Asia* (Boston, 1907).
CHILDE, V. GORDON. *The Aryans* (London, 1926).
CHILDE, V. GORDON. *The Dawn of European Civilization* (London, 1925)
PEAKE, HAROLD. *The Bronze Age and the Celtic World* (London, 1922).

4

New Arrivals in Greece

IT is to about 2600 B.C. that we must attribute the evidence of a fresh culture in the unforested country of Eastern Thessaly. The new people, responsible for this fresh culture, lived in fortified settlements, that remind us of the village of Cucuteni, but in Thessaly several sets of ditches and ramparts are found some little distance apart from one another.

The best preserved of these fortifications are at Dhimini, where they consist of a series of ring walls, of only moderate height, but providing successive lines of defence, between which lay a narrow and tortuous alley, the only approach to the centre of the village. Remains of a similar series were discovered at Sesklo, but these would have been difficult to interpret without the more complete scheme at Dhimini as a guide. It is probable that other similarly defended villages existed in Eastern Thessaly, but, if we may judge by the pottery, not in the western part of that area, much of which was then densely wooded. Fortified villages of this type, though probably of later date, have been found in several of the Aegean islands, at Khalandriani in Syros, Agio Andreas in Siphnos, and at Phylakopi in Melos. We shall meet them, too, elsewhere farther north in Europe.

The new-comers introduced the porched house or megaron, a type of building that we have already met with at Erösd. This is rectangular in its plan, and consists, as a rule, of two rooms, one lying behind the other, while there is a porch at one end of the building; this porch was usually supported by wooden pillars. The hearth was sometimes in the middle of the front room, at others against the partition wall. Such houses were used at a later date in Greece, and Homer gives us descriptions of similar dwellings in the Odyssey. It is thought that it was from buildings of this type that the Doric temples of Classical Greece were derived.

These people used a great variety of pottery, known, from the

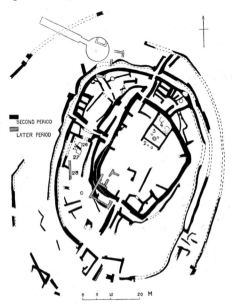

SECOND PERIOD
LATER PERIOD

FIG. 23. Dhimini; plan after Tsountas.

site at which it was first discovered, as Dhimini ware. The shape and decoration of this ware, painted in several colours and decorated with spirals and meanders, remind us of that discovered at Cucuteni, and still more of the pottery found at Erösd. We can have no doubt, therefore, that the makers of this ware had come from somewhere in the Black Earth region.

The new-comers made figurines of earthenware, not quite

so good as those made by their predecessors, but these were perforated for suspension; they also made clay models of cattle. A few fiddle-pattern stone figurines, found in some of their settlements, were most probably brought from the Cyclades, and perhaps came in by way of trade.

Like their predecessors, the new-comers were growers of

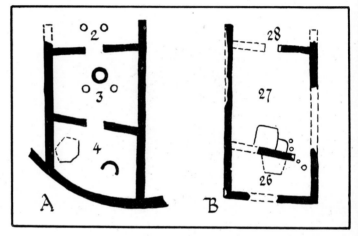

FIG. 24. Megara at Dhimini, after Tsountas.

grain and used shoe-last celts for hoes, but during this period a fresh type of celt with a thicker butt came into use; unlike their fore-runners they were acquainted with the use of metal. It is believed that their predecessors, like the early peasants in the Danube basin, had cultivated einkorn, an inferior type of wheat that grows wild in Asia Minor and in many parts of Greece. In a deposit of this second period at Sesklo, Tsountas found grains that have been identified as the bread wheat (*Triticum vulgare*), which seems to have been introduced by these new-comers from the South Russian Plain.

A small ring pendant of gold was found at Sesklo, while
triangular daggers, awls, and a bracelet, all of copper, were
found farther south at Hagia Marina in Phocis, in a settlement
of this period, though not of this culture. The occurrence of
barbed arrow-heads of copper as well as of flint shows that they
introduced the use of the bow. Another innovation was the

FIG. 25. Bowl from Dhimini, after Tsountas.

use of buttons with V perforations; these we shall meet with
again in Central and Western Europe.

The close resemblance of all these new features to those that
we have found earlier at the villages of Cucuteni and Erösd,
which we described in *Priests & Kings*, leaves us in no doubt
that the new-comers into Thessaly hailed from the Black Earth
region, and the occasional occurrence of objects of this type in
Bulgaria and Thrace points to the route by which they arrived.

Whether they were refugees, driven from their former homes
by the ochre-grave folk from the steppe, or whether they were
carried to Thessaly as slaves or subjects by these warlike nomads,
is a doubtful point. Childe holds to the former view. In support of the latter we may cite the bows and arrows that they
brought with them, weapons more suitable to the nomads than

to the peaceful peasants of the Black Earth. A skull from a deposit of this period at Tsangli, with a length-breadth index of 76·9 and a very high nose, suggests that some of the ochre-

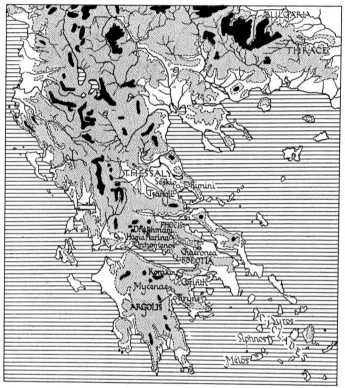

FIG. 26. Map of Thessaly and adjoining regions.

grave people came too, and, if so, almost certainly as rulers. This question must, however, remain undecided for the present.

Farther to the west, especially on the wooded slopes of the mountains, the old civilization continued as before, undisturbed by the new-comers. It spread also southwards towards Central Greece, where settlements grew up at Drakhmani, Hagia Marina, Chaeronea, and Orchomenos, in the basin of the Cephissus. Further settlements were made in Boeotia and in the

FIG. 27. Fragments of ware, believed to be Danubian, from Tiryns.

neighbourhood of Corinth, where remains of this civilization have been found at Korakou.

It would seem that it was not long after the arrival of the steppe-folk in the Danube basin that some of the previous peasant inhabitants moved southwards. These appear to have passed up the Morava and down the Vardar Valley, and thus to have reached the north of Thessaly. Here they seem to have arrived not very long after the appearance of the people from the Black Earth Lands. At any rate, at a date which cannot be much later than that at which the Dhimini pottery first appeared in the east of Thessaly, we find pots of spiral-meander ware, typical of the First Danubian civilization, turning up on the sites in the west of Thessaly. Thus, during the period under review, we have two cultural provinces in Thessaly. On the east a culture from the Black Earth Lands, possibly dominated by men from the steppe; on the west settlements of the aborigines, reinforced by refugees from the Danube basin.

The Danubian refugees passed southwards to the settlements in Phocis and Boeotia, made by the first Thessalian peasants, and, like the latter, ultimately reached the Gulf of Corinth. Fragments of pottery, which Frankfort believes to be of their spiral-meander ware, have even been found as far south as Tiryns.

Thus the primitive peasants from Thessaly and the Danube basin were in peaceable possession, not only of Western Thessaly, but of the rich valley of the Cephissus and the head of the Corinthian Gulf. They had even ventured as far south as the Plain of Argolis, but they were not to be left long in undisputed possession of all the richest lands in the peninsula.

It would seem that it was about 2800 B.C. that traders from the Cyclades landed on the coast of Argolis and settled first at Tiryns and then at Mycenae, for at these places we find in the lowest deposit the primitive glazed ware characteristic of those islands. Here they built round houses. These people at a later date advanced to Corinth, the foundation of which seems to be due to them, and settled among the peasants around the head of the gulf. About the same time they landed on the coast of Phocis, and seem to have made themselves masters of Orchomenos, for their primitive glazed ware predominates in the second layer on

that site. Here they built oval houses, or rectangular houses
with a semicircular end. From the coast of Phocis they seem to
have kept up a trade with neighbouring lands, for objects from
Hissarlik have been found in the second layer of Orchomenos,
which belongs to this time.

BOOKS

CHILDE, V. GORDON. *The Dawn of European Civilization* (London, 1925).
WACE, A. J. B. and THOMPSON, M. S. *Prehistoric Thessaly* (Cambridge,
    1912).

5

The Spread of the Peasants

WE have seen that there is good reason for believing that the
ochre-grave people from the Russian steppe, after destroying
the settlements in the Black Earth region, passed on into the
Danube basin and made themselves masters over the peasant
settlements on the Hungarian Plain. Having been accustomed
to a life spent in hunting and in herding cattle, it is unlikely
that they took kindly to agricultural operations; it seems more
probable that they made themselves lords over the peasant
population, leaving them to cultivate the soil, while they under-
took the task of governing and of defending the settlements
from the incursions of wild beasts or of such as remained of the
Epipalaeolithic hunters. It is interesting to remember that in
the rural life of Europe the waste and the hunting rights down
to our own time have typically belonged to the 'lords' in a very
special and intimate way.

    Soon after the arrival of these nomads within the Carpathian
ring, perhaps even before they had made their power felt
throughout the whole region, the peasants on the margin,
especially on the west and in the north-west corner, began to
spread farther afield, the former passing up the Danube Valley

through Austria into Bavaria, the latter westwards into Bohemia and north-eastwards through the Moravian gap. The distributions of forest and loess had a great deal to do with the directions of these movements.

Of those that passed through the gap, some turned eastwards into Galicia and settled on the loess patches at the northern foot of the Carpathian Mountains; these met some of the ochregrave people who had arrived here from the Russian steppe,

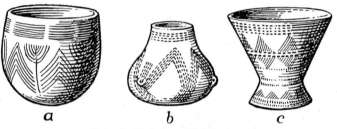

FIG. 28. Vases from Hinkelstein.

and, in all probability, refugees from the 'Black Earth' settlements around Horodnica. Others travelled down the Oder Valley as far as Nosswitz in Silesia, where remains of huts, containing pottery of the spiral-meander type, were found beneath a later settlement. From Bohemia other peasants spread down the Elbe Valley as far as Magdeburg.

From Saxony some of these peasants, still using the strokeornamented pottery described in the preceding volume of this series, crossed the Thuringian Mountains into the Neckar Valley. Down this valley they moved, selecting the patches of loess, relatively free from trees, for the purpose of cultivation, and at length reached the valley of the Rhine; here their most important settlements have been found in the neighbourhood of Worms. A large cemetery of these people has been excavated at Hinkelstein near that city, but among the remains found there were some vases with expanded feet, like that in figure 28 *c*, and shoe-last celts with perforations; both of these are features of the Second Danubian civilization. These details and the presence in the cemetery of skeletons of tall men with long heads suggest that by the time that the peasants had reached the Rhine, they had been overtaken by the conquerors from the Russian steppe.

Another group of peasants in Saxony developed a new type of pottery, which has features that remind us both of the stroke-

FIG. 29. Pottery of the Rössen type.

ornamented and the spiral-meander wares. It is best represented by specimens found in the cemetery at Rössen in the neighbour-hood of Merseburg, which lies on the Saale just south of Halle. This pottery is found extending from the Saale eastwards to the Elbe. The vases found at Rössen have feet and are decorated with deep strokes encrusted with white paste; these features seem to imply that some, at any rate, of the peasant makers of the ware had not left the Danube basin until some little time after the beginning of the Second Danubian period in that region. The people were buried in a slightly contracted position, but towards the close of the period the practice of cremation was introduced.

From Rössen and the valley of the Saale some of these

peasants passed westwards across Hesse to the head-waters of
the Sieg, and down the valley of that river to the Rhine, opposite
to Bonn. In passing through the hill country between the Saale
and the Rhine, they seem to have depended for food less than
hitherto upon grain and domesticated animals, and to have
reverted to some extent to their former hunting condition, for
among the remains left at their settlements the bones of wild
animals exceed in numbers those of domesticated kinds.

Another group of peasants, using the spiral-meander type
of pottery, passed up the Danube and ultimately reached the
middle basin of the Rhine. These seem to have kept free from
other influences, for they had not even adopted the strokeornamented ware, the shape and decoration of which were
copied, so we have suggested, from the leather bags of the
Epipalaeolithic hunters. Their civilization had been very little
affected by that of the ochre-grave nomads from the Russian
steppe, though occasionally they placed lumps of red ochre in
their graves. They continued to import *Spondylus* shells from
the Aegean Sea, and still buried their dead in a contracted
position. Their settlements on the Rhine have been found in
the neighbourhood of Mainz, the best known of them being at
Flomborn, from which their type of civilization takes its name.
Ultimately the Flomborn and the Hinkelstein civilizations
coalesced, and gave rise to a third, known as the Plaidt civilization, so called from the place in the Eifel Mountains where it
was first discovered.

Another group of peasants, passing up the Danube Valley a
little later than the Flomborn people, settled at Münchshofen,
which lies a few miles south of the river about half-way between
Regensburg and Passau. Here they were joined by others, who
had started later from the Hungarian Plain and had brought
with them some elements of the Second Danubian civilization.
These developed a special type of pottery, known as Münchs-

hofen ware. From this neighbourhood, as we shall see, some of these peasants moved southwards to the lakes at the foot of the Bavarian Alps.

Other peasants seem to have left the south-eastern corner of the Middle Danube basin and passed up the valley of the Save, and up that of its tributary the Bosna, to the neighbourhood of Sarajevo, where a settlement has been discovered on the moors around Butmir. Here have been found the spiral decoration, shoe-last celts, and disk-shaped mace-heads, all suggestive of the

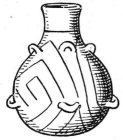

FIG. 30. Pottery from Flomborn.

First Danubian civilization. The presence also of footed bowls and white encrusted pottery suggests that the people of Butmir had not left their original home until some little time after the beginning of the Second Danubian period. At Butmir, as at all the sites mentioned in this chapter, no signs of metal were found.

It should be realized that metal-working involves considerable organization and well-developed communications, especially if it is to get beyond mere copper work, and copper pure and simple was an advance on stone only for particular purposes. Peasant communities spreading step by step, sometimes moving as mere refugees, would hardly have the organized communications needed to supply metal to any large area; a good deal of this organization was very probably developed under the influence of the conquering horsemen from the steppe. These may have contributed a great deal indirectly to the spread of the art of bronze working, though they may not have done it themselves; indeed this last possibility is an unlikely one.

Fig. 31. Münchshofen ware.

In due course the steppe people seem to have followed these wandering peasants into Silesia and Saxony and, later on, into Bavaria, for in these places we find settlements bearing all the characteristics of the Second Danubian civilization. The most important of the sites, at which this second phase appears, are

Ottitz and Jordansmühl in Silesia, besides, as we have seen, Münchshofen in Bavaria. Ultimately the Danubian civilization, sometimes, however, free from Second Danubian influence, spread up and down the Rhine from the Jura to Cologne.

Fig. 32. Pottery from Butmir.

It seems probable that these Danubian peasants did not cease from wandering when they reached the valley of the Rhine, for their methods of cultivation were primitive and they were ignorant of the importance of having a rotation of crops, and it is even doubtful whether they realized the value of manure. It was essential, therefore, if they were to obtain a good return for their labours, that they should constantly bring under cultivation fresh patches of virgin soil. With their stone

E

axes it was not easy to clear the forest, even with the aid of fire;
they were therefore constantly on the move in search of open
spaces with soil suitable for agriculture. Up till now no very
certain evidence of their presence west of the Rhine Valley has
come to light, except in one district; but this may be due in

Fig. 33. Omalian pottery from La Hesbaye.

great measure to the fact that it has not been sought for. Some
Spondylus shells have, however, been discovered in the outskirts
of Paris, so we may expect shortly to find traces of their presence
in the valley of the Seine.

In one region, indeed, clear evidence has been found of early
agricultural communities, which can be shown by the decoration
on their pottery to be of Danubian origin. This is in La Hesbaye,
a district in Belgium lying immediately west of the Meuse,
between Liége and Brussels. Remains of one such settlement

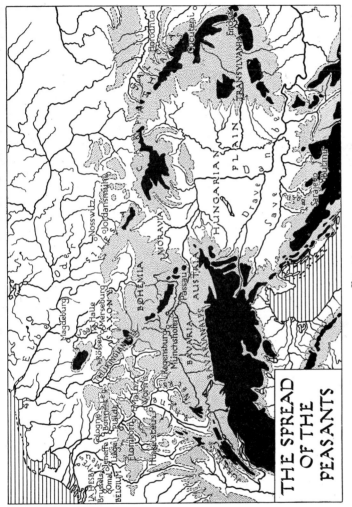

THE SPREAD
OF THE
PEASANTS

Fig. 34.

were actually discovered beneath the market place at Liége, which enables us to pronounce that city to be one of the oldest, if not actually the oldest permanent settlement in North-west Europe. In this district, on a soil allied to loess, a large number of agricultural settlements have been traced, with pottery clearly derived from the spiral-meander ware of Moravia. The first settlement was found at Omal, near Brussels, so that their civilization has sometimes been called Omalian. Another settlement has lately been found at Caberg in Holland.

It seems probable that some of the peasants who had settled near Worms, or more probably some of those from the neighbourhood of Flomborn, had passed down the valley of the Rhine and skirted the northern foot-hills of the Eifel until they reached the neighbourhood of Liége. Here they had spread out over a limited area of loess. Beyond that on all sides they found long stretches of light soil, reaching as far as the North Sea, much of it covered with dunes and loose drifting sands. This they thought unsuitable for cultivation, so they proceeded no farther in this direction.

The presence of pottery and settled habitations made it clear to the discoverers of the Omalian settlements that their occupants had been grain growers; but at Jeneffe M. de Puydt found some grain that was pronounced by M. A. Gravis to be emmer, an identification since confirmed by Professor Percival. This is somewhat surprising, for, as we have seen, the First Danubian peasants are thought to have cultivated einkorn, while bread wheat (*T. vulgare*) was introduced from the Black Earth region at the beginning of the Second Danubian period. Emmer is found mainly in Syria and Egypt and was thence disseminated throughout the Mediterranean lands. The occurrence of emmer in La Hesbaye with relics of Omalian civilization seems to indicate that by this time sea-borne influences had already reached the north-western shores of Europe.

In our preceding volume we saw that the first growers of grain to arrive in the south-east corner of the Middle Danube basin were well acquainted with metal, and were probably mining both copper and gold in south-east Hungary and Transylvania. Those, however, who had migrated to Moravia had lost the art of metallurgy. The emigrants whose wanderings we have been tracing in this chapter had no knowledge of metal, though they had retained the practice of growing grain and kept a few domesticated animals. They were, in the strict sense of the term, in a Neolithic state of culture, and it is now becoming increasingly certain that all that we know as Neolithic culture in Europe was derived from the spread of Danubian civilization, or of some other influences derived from regions in which gold and copper had long been known.

BOOKS

CHILDE, V. GORDON. *The Dawn of European Civilization* (London, 1925).

6

The Lake-dwellers of Central Europe

IT was in the winter of 1853 and 1854 that, owing to a period of drought, a discovery was made which was interpreted as showing that the early inhabitants of Switzerland had lived in houses and villages erected on piles in the shallow waters of the lakes or on the marshy lands adjoining them. In later years similar structures were found on Lakes Annecy and Bourget and elsewhere in Savoy, at Aichbühl and other sites near Schussenried in Württemberg, by Attersee and Mondsee in Austria, and at Ljubljano, formerly called Laibach, in Carniola; settlements of a closely allied type were discovered later by the shores of the Italian lakes, Maggiore and Garda. These settlements were found to date from the Neolithic, Bronze, and Early Iron Ages, and in some cases came to an end only shortly before the conquest of that region by the Romans.

A relative chronology for the later settlements was easily constructed, but those of the Neolithic Age presented greater difficulties. They were arranged in a sequence depending upon the type of pottery used, those with the rougher wares being placed earlier than those in which finer vases had been found. The Neolithic Age here was divided into three periods; these were known as the Archaic (Wauwil, Moosseedorf, &c.), the Robenhausen (Concise, &c.), and the Morgienne (Morges, Locraz or in German Lüscherz, &c.). Since Herodotus mentions similar dwellings in Paeonia, adjoining Macedonia, and as Hippocrates states that others existed in Asia Minor, it was assumed that the practice of erecting such structures had been brought from the East; this view was supported by the discovery in these villages of fruits that grow wild in Armenia.

During a long spell of dry weather in the summer of 1921 the level of the Lake of Neuchâtel sank by several feet and the sites of some of these lake villages were left dry. Advantage was taken of this opportunity by M. Paul Vouga, who excavated some of these sites, where he found several superimposed deposits. From this stratification he was able to determine a number of successive stages of civilization, the lowest three of which contained no metal; these he termed the Early, Middle, and Upper Neolithic stages. Contrary to what had up to that time been believed, he found that the finest pottery came from the lowest and oldest layer, and that it degenerated steadily throughout the later periods. The wares belonging to the earliest period were of fine quality and bear an unmistakable likeness to some types of Second Danubian pottery. It is not yet possible, however, to determine with precision the relations between this classification and that formerly used.

The pottery of the Early Neolithic stratum is of much the same type throughout the north-east of Switzerland, and these wares, especially those found by the shores of Lake Constance, resemble very closely the pottery found in the bottom layer at Aichbühl on the Federsee moor in Württemberg by Dr. Hans Reinerth and Professor R. R. Schmidt. The pottery from this

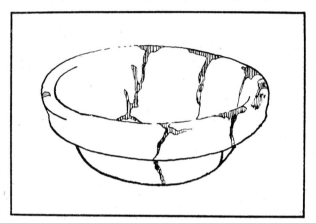

FIG. 35. Early Neolithic Pottery from Port-Conty.

last site has undoubted affinities with the Münchshofen ware, the Bavarian variety of the Second Danubian pottery.

Though some of the chief elements of the Early Neolithic civilization of the lake-dwellers have thus been derived from Danubian sources, including not only the pottery but the art of agriculture and the possession of domesticated animals, there are other features which did not belong to the culture of the Danubian peasants. For instance the earliest lake-dwellers on Lake Neuchâtel had painted pebbles, very like those found at Mas d'Azil; they seem to have painted themselves with red ochre like the Azilians, and wore boars' tusks with perforations at both ends. Sometimes they wore as amulets fragments of human skull, acquired by trepanning, and there is more than a suspicion that they practised cannibalism. Other objects found in the lowest layer of these deposits, such as picks, horn sleeves for mounting axes, harpoons, horn fish-spears, and other objects, can be closely paralleled from the Baltic settlements at Magle-mose and Brabrand, which have been described in *Hunters and Artists*, the second part of this series. It is clear, therefore, that the culture of the Danubian peasants had been grafted on to that of the epipalaeolithic descendants of the men of Ofnet, and there is some ground for thinking that these people had been joined by visitors coming up the Rhine from Denmark or the shores of the North Sea, before the Danubian peasants had appeared in this region. Dr. von Fellenberg has stated that some of the flint found in the lake-dwellings has come from the island of Rügen in the Baltic; if this is so, this material must have been brought thither by these visitors from the north.

The origin of the pile-dwellings is obscure. In some cases the earlier settlements deserve this name, for they were buildings erected on platforms, which rested on piles driven into the mud. In other cases, however, the dwellings were on another sort of platform, a kind of stack of logs laid on marshy soil near the lake. The latter type are the more common on the Rhine, from Schaffhausen downwards, but they occur also on the margins of the Swiss lakes.

Childe has suggested tentatively that these platforms may have been derived from the rafts on which the Maglemose people made their settlements. He has pointed out that such rafts, or platforms derived from them, were used near Stock-holm by descendants of the Maglemose people, whose culture is known as Arctic, quite as late as the period in which the Swiss lake-dwellings began to be constructed. If we could be sure that all, or even any, of the platforms preceded the earliest pile-

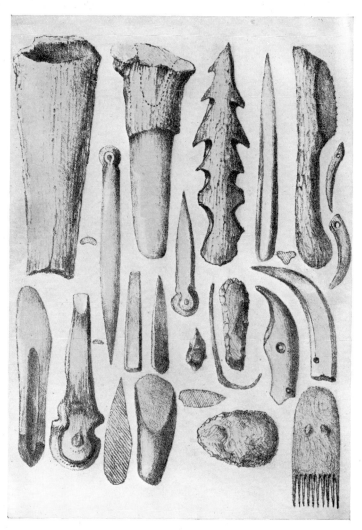

Fig. 36. Horn objects from Moosseedorf.

dwellings, this explanation would be almost, if not quite, conclusive. Unfortunately, however, some of the true pile-dwellings contain objects apparently quite as early as any found on the platforms, so we must leave this explanation of the origin of the lake-dwellings as a plausible but as yet unproved hypothesis.

The people of the lake-dwellings lived, as we have seen, in wooden houses, erected upon a structure of piles, driven into the muddy margins of the lake, or occasionally upon platforms constructed of layers of trunks laid crosswise one upon another. The houses were made of tree trunks placed vertically close together, and consisted of two rooms, with a porch at one end, which reminds us of the megaron at Erösd and those at Dhimini.

Even the earliest of these lake-dwellers were cultivators of grain, but until the older sites have been brought into relation with those excavated in 1920–1 by Vouga at Auvernier, Cortaillod, and at Port-Conty in the Commune of Saint-Aubin on Lake Neuchâtel, we cannot be sure what species of grain were grown in his earliest period. At Robenhausen, which belongs to the second Neolithic period of the old scheme, barley and three kinds of wheat, Einkorn, Emmer, and Bread Wheat, were grown; while at Wangen, which was placed in the same period, another kind of barley was grown as well as two species of wheat, Emmer and Bread Wheat. Millet was also grown at Wangen, while flax was cultivated at most of the early sites. We have seen that Einkorn was probably grown by the Early Danubians, and that the Bread Wheat was introduced from South Russia at the beginning of the Second Danubian period; Emmer, however, was not grown in south-east Europe, and was probably introduced into Switzerland from the south or the west.

The same difficulty meets us with domesticated animals. The large ox (*Bos primigenius*), almost certainly hunted wild, has been reported from Sutz of the third, and from Font of the

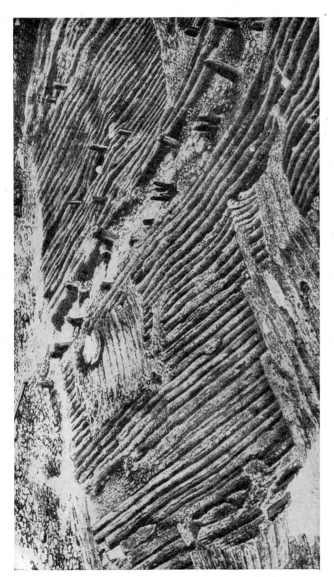

Fig. 37. Stacked platform from Lake Niederwyl (Egelsee).

fourth period, according to the old classification; the short-horned ox (*Bos brachyceros*) from Lattrigen, Schafis, and Vinelz, of the third period; and a hornless ox from Sutz. The wild marsh pig was found at Lattrigen, Moosseedorf, and Wauwil, the

Fig. 38. Reconstruction of Neolithic Pile-dwellings at Unter Uhldingen on Lake Constance, after R. R. Schmidt.   *Photograph by Dr. Douglas Guthrie.*

last two sites belonging to the first or Archaic period. The goat was found at Sutz and Vinelz, and the sheep at Font and Schaffis.

The pottery found by Vouga in the lowest layer was a fine dark grey ware with perforated protuberances. The stone implements were made of a dark translucent flint, which was not found in the upper layers. These were let into 'sleeves' or sockets of stag antler, with no shoulder, such as is found in later deposits. These characters should enable students on the spot to identify the periods to which should be relegated the settlements found in earlier years, but so far the only conclusions on this point that have been published are by Dr. Hans Reinerth. He relegates to the first period the settlements at Guévaux in

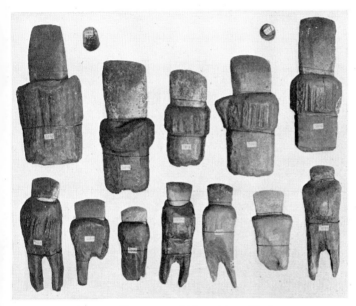

FIG. 39. Three types of 'sleeves' from Vinelz.

Canton Vaud, Greng in Canton Fribourg, Moosseedorf in Canton Berne, Ober-Siggingen in Canton Aargau, Richensee, Schötz, and Wauwil in Canton Lucerne, Steckborn and Thurberg-Weinfelden in Canton Thurgau. Vouga, on the other hand, states that the dark grey pottery that he met with in the bottom layer at Auvernier had not previously been found in the Neuchâtel region.

A series of antler 'sleeves' from Vinelz, published by Tschumi,

shows only one without and the remainder with the shoulder, which suggests that this settlement is later than Vouga's Early Neolithic period; it was placed in the third period by earlier writers. On the other hand, Keller figures two shoulderless sleeves from Meilen, which Schenk placed in the third or

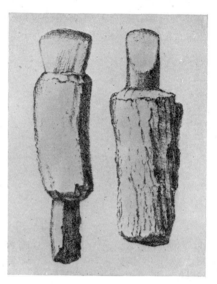

FIG. 40. Two shoulderless sleeves from Meilen.

Morgienne period, and a shouldered sleeve from Wauwil, which Schenk placed in his first or Archaic period. A bone comb and some clay loom-weights show us that weaving was practised.

It will be seen that it is at present very difficult to describe with accuracy the state of civilization that obtained during Vouga's Early Neolithic period, the only one with which we are at present concerned, and the origin of the various elements of this culture and of the type of people responsible for them are equally obscure. It seems probable, as already stated, that Switzerland and the adjoining regions had been inhabited for long by people of the Ofnet type, who had been joined by other epipalaeolithic folk from the west, and had gleaned a little of the idea of pottery, as we shall try to show in the next volume. Very possibly they were joined, too, by fresh arrivals from the north, who had ascended the Rhine from the coast of the North Sea, which we know was well within the area of the Maglemose

Fig. 41. Perforated stag-antler hammers from Meilen.

culture. Besides several cultural items already referred to, such as the horizontal platform of tree trunks, we may attribute to these intruders from the north the introduction of perforated hammers, made from the butt end of a deer's antler, for such have been found in many of the lake villages.

Lastly, some Danubian peasants, or hunting peoples who had come into contact with these peasants farther to the east and had learned their culture, came up the Danube basin to the neighbourhood of Münchshofen, and arrived at the foot of the Bavarian Alps at a date which cannot be earlier than 2500 B.C., and may well be later. Thence they spread east and west. In the south-west they reached Lake Constance and passed thence southwards to the Zürich region and south-westwards to Lake

Neuchâtel, Lake Geneva, and the Lakes of Savoy. Eastwards they spread to the Mondsee and the Attersee and ultimately round the mountain zone to Laibach Moor. Later, probably after metal was known to them, some of them crossed the Brenner Pass into Italy and settled at the southern end of the Lago di Garda, while others, perhaps, passed thence along the foot-hills of the Alps to Lago Maggiore, unless the inhabitants of that part had moved up the Rhone Valley from Lake Geneva and crossed the Simplon Pass.

It has been suggested by some writers that many of the elements of culture reached Switzerland from the west, from France and from Spain; and the presence of Emmer at some of the Neolithic sites is suggestive of such a connexion, for Emmer was first cultivated in the Mediterranean region. On the other hand, the chief items of evidence that such writers depend on are axes of jadeite, which are believed to have come from Brittany, and implements of honey-coloured or beeswax flint, which are known to have been derived from Le Grand Pressigny in the Department of Indre-et-Loire. Vouga, however, found no Grand Pressigny flint in his lower layers; it appeared first in his fourth, which also contained objects of copper. On the other hand, Vouga states that pottery resembling his dark grey ware has been found at Le Camp de Chassey in the Department of Saône-et-Loire, which suggests an east to west movement. As we shall try to show in the next volume, two movements met in Switzerland about this time, one from the east and the other from the west.

BOOKS

CHILDE, V. GORDON. *The Dawn of European Civilization* (London, 1925).

BURKITT, M. C. *Our Early Ancestors* (Cambridge, 1926).

MUNRO, R. *The Lake Dwellings of Europe.* (London, 1890).

KELLER, F. *The Lake Dwellings of Switzerland.* (Transl. J. E. Lee).

MUNRO, R. *Palaeolithic Man and Terramara Settlements in Europe.* 1912.

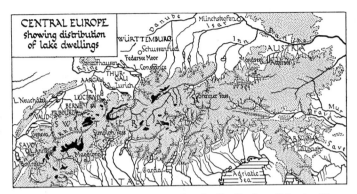

Fig. 42. Map of Central Europe showing the distribution of lake-dwellings.

Fig. 43. Large pieces of beeswax flint from Grand Pressigny.
(After Henri Martin.)

7

Maritime Activity in the Aegean

WE have seen in the preceding volume of this series that bowls of syenite, porphyry, and diorite, made in styles that were current in Egypt during the Old Kingdom, and even during the Second Dynasty, have been found in Crete; this indicates that during the early part of the third millennium this island had already entered into commercial relations with the Valley of the Nile. It is generally believed that this intercourse was carried on by Cretans rather than by Egyptians. Thus maritime activity appears as a prime factor of Aegean civilization.

It is important to note, too, that Melos, one of the Cycladic Isles, had stores of obsidian, which from the very early stages of the Aegean civilization had been used in many other islands as well as on the mainland in Thessaly; this demonstrates the existence of maritime intercourse and probably organized trade. Cyprus also, probably well before 3000 B.C., had already established relations with other places; these brought to it influences from the old Sumerian civilization of Mesopotamia. We cannot but connect the rise to importance of this island in those early times with its rich veins of copper. It is said to have been uninhabited in earlier times.

Thus in the first half of the third millennium there was a considerable stirring of maritime life in the Eastern Mediterranean, and we may well imagine that great progress was already being made towards the building of those narrow, high-prowed ships with long oars that we find depicted on the Cretan pots of a later date.

The isles of the Cyclades yield interesting products; obsidian is to be found in Melos, copper and marble in Paros, while emery occurs in Naxos. On this account it seems that they, like Cyprus, were brought early into the circle of this maritime civilization. Some believe that at first they were unpeopled, and that for some centuries they were visited by traders rather than fully

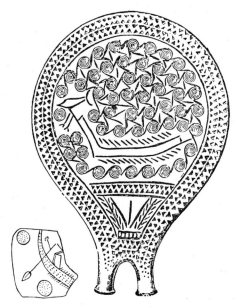

Fig. 44. Cycladic sherd and 'frying-pan' depicting boats.

inhabited, and that no regular settlements were made upon them until about 2800 B.C. Frankfort, however, is of opinion that they were inhabited long before 3000 B.C. Voyagers among these islands could use the alternate land and sea breezes in spring, or might venture out in the summer days, exposing themselves to the Etesian winds from the north, and thus sail from the Cyclades to Crete and thence to Egypt. With the very simple boats used in early days navigation during the winter would have been perilous and wellnigh impossible, except for short distances; this was, in all probability, the chief factor that delayed the growth of settlements on the smaller islands.

Though a somewhat earlier settlement of rude huts had

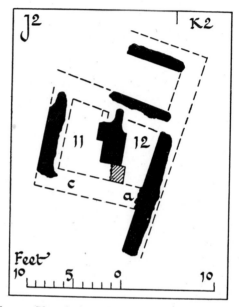

FIG. 45. Plan of a house in the First City of Phylakopi.
(After T. D. Atkinson.)

existed there, it was about 2400 B.C., at the beginning of the Third Early Cycladic period, that a permanent city of some size was established at Phylakopi in the island of Melos. Here the first city contained houses with a number of rectangular rooms, built of stone, at any rate in the lower layers. It was unfortified, showing that the inhabitants considered that their island home was not liable to attack. A somewhat later city at

Khalandriani, on the island of Syros, was surrounded by a double line of wall, which seems to tell us that these peaceful conditions did not long continue, unless we may understand that this later settlement was made by refugees from the mainland, who had not yet realized the security of an island home.

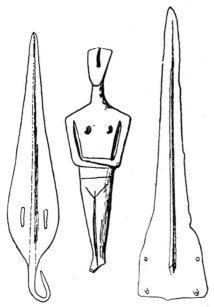

Fig. 46. Tomb group from Amorgos. Scale 2 : 9.

The chief article of export from Melos was obsidian, and during the period under review large stocks of half-finished implements were exported to other lands. So long as copper was the only metal used for making tools, this natural volcanic glass, which takes a keen edge, was much in demand. At the time of the First City of Phylakopi the obsidian industry was already waning, for a better material for tools was already coming on the

market. It had been discovered that by adding a certain proportion of tin to copper a much harder alloy could be produced,
and already the people of the Cyclades were importing silver,
lead, and tin. That they were trading with Cyprus at the time is
clear from the presence in a tomb on the island of Amorgos of
a typical Cypriote blade, together with a figurine which belongs
undoubtedly to this period.

We have seen, too, that about 3000 B. C., or perhaps even
earlier, a grain-growing people, using painted pots, had arrived
in Thessaly; these used obsidian tools, which seem to have been
obtained from Melos, and stone hoes, of the type known as
shoe-last celts, which closely resemble those used in the Danube
basin. It is thus clear that Thessaly had some trade relations
with the islands of the Aegean. By 2400 B. C. the Cycladic folk
had settled on the mainland of Greece, in the Plain of Argolis,
where their civilization is known as Helladic.

This Aegean civilization had not developed very far when
there occurred, between 2600 and 2500 B. C., the disturbances
already described in previous chapters. The nomadic people
of the South Russian steppe destroyed the civilization that had
grown up in the Black Earth region, and we can hardly doubt
but that the effects of this irruption must have been felt
throughout the whole Aegean region. At the same time, as we
shall see in later chapters, similar irruptions of folk from the
steppes and deserts had caused the downfall of the Mesopotamian Empire founded by Sargon of Agade, and brought to
an abrupt end the civilization of the Old Kingdom in Egypt.

The study of the graves of the Donetz valley has shown us
that some of the steppe-folk had had trade connexions with the
Cyclades, or with some port in Asia Minor in close touch with
these islands, while the tombs in the Kuban Valley contain
metal objects that are clearly of Mesopotamian origin, or have
been made under Mesopotamian influences. How such influ-

ences reached South Russia at so early a date is uncertain, though we may conjecture that they passed across Asia Minor.

FIG. 47. Clay tablet from Boghaz Keui in the Halys basin.

Near the village of Kaṛa Euyuk in the Halys Valley, right in the heart of Asia Minor, was an early settlement of Sumerian traders.

Clay tablets, containing records of their business transactions, have been found there by Hrozný, and we know from these that Sumerian merchants were collecting both wool and metals from or beyond and dispatching them to Mesopotamia as early as 2100 B.C. How early this trading-post arose is at present uncertain, but the unsettled condition of the Sumerian cities after the reign of Dungi, king of Ur, who died in 2393 B.C., makes it unlikely that the settlement was first established after that date. It seems more likely that the foundation of this place goes back to the time of Sargon, king of Agade from 2752 to 2697 B.C., for we know that a considerable expansion of trade, especially to the north-west, took place during his reign.

It seems likely, then, that a line of trade passed from North Syria through the Cilician gorge to the Halys basin and passed thence to the southern shores of the Black Sea; a farther route around the eastern end of that sea would bring traders, without meeting any serious obstacle on the way, to the mouth of the Kuban river.

We have shown in our preceding volume that the empire of Sargon of Agade stretched from the Persian Gulf to the Mediterranean coast of Syria, and that beyond the latter were Kaphtor and Ku-ki. Kaphtor was undoubtedly Crete, and it has been suggested that Ku-ki was Cyprus. Whether this identification be correct or not, there is little doubt that Cyprus was at this time in touch with the civilization of Mesopotamia.

We know very little about Asia Minor in these early days, but the evidence we have cited tends to show that from this region the elements of civilization, derived, in great measure at least, from Mesopotamia and Syria, spread in all directions. Sir Arthur Evans has pointed out how the earliest civilization in Crete seems to be derived from that country, and we have given reasons, in the preceding volume of this series, for believing that the civilizations of the Cyclades, Thessaly, and the Danube

Fig. 48. Pottery of the Third Early Cycladic period.

basin were derived from the same region. We must attribute to the same source many of the elements of civilization of the Kuban Valley and the Black Earth region as well as that of Anau in Turkestan.

On the other hand, as Sir Arthur Evans has repeatedly shown, Crete was in direct contact with Egypt and perhaps, too, with other parts of the North African coast, so that there was a complete network of trade, connecting together all the civilized parts of the world. Much of this commerce seems to have been conducted by land, across Asia Minor and around the Black Sea, but even from very early days some of the connexions, notably those between the Cyclades, Crete, and the Nile Valley, were carried on in favourable weather by sea.

The disturbances on land, caused by the activities of the various steppe peoples, made overland ventures difficult and hazardous, and the markets of Egypt, Mesopotamia, and the Black Earth region were cut off. This gave a fresh impetus to sea-borne traffic, which was as yet safe from attacks by the steppe-folk, and caused the Aegean peoples to seek new markets and to search for fresh supplies of the raw materials that they needed. Land traffic, although interrupted for a time, was, as we shall see, resumed in due course along fresh trade routes. To meet these new conditions two centres of activity developed in importance, Crete and Hissarlik, and to these we must now turn our attention.

BOOKS

CHILDE, V. GORDON. *The Dawn of European Civilization* (London, 1925).

8

The Second City of Hissarlik

THE northern half of the Aegean Sea did not lend itself so
well to very early maritime activities as the southern part, the
sea that lies between the Cyclades and around the islands of
Crete and Rhodes. The islands are fewer and lie farther apart,
while the force of the Etesian wind is greater. It is natural,
therefore, to find that the chief centres of culture in this region
lie on the mainland rather than on islands.

A low hill, lying in the middle of a broad valley in the north-
western corner of Asia Minor, is the site of the city of Troy,
destroyed by the Achaeans in 1184 B.C. It had for some centuries
been a city of vast importance, and it was the sixth settlement
upon the mound of Hissarlik.

The third, fourth, and fifth settlements were apparently of
comparatively small importance, but their predecessor, the
Second City, was a great centre of intercourse until it was burnt
down not long after 2000 B.C.

Relatively little is known of the first settlement, called
Hissarlik I, the remains of which lie under those of Hissarlik
II. The latter city is so important that every effort is being
made to study its remains before undermining parts of it to
investigate more fully the first settlement. What is known up
to the present of the earlier village has been summarized in the
preceding volume of this series.

There are important veins of silver in the mountains that lie
at the back of Hissarlik, and it is possible that the existence of
these in the neighbourhood may have been one of the factors
that led to the growth of importance of the site. On the other
hand, its geographical position, lying as it does near the narrow
channel that divides two continents, may, as we shall see later,

have had more to do with the growth of its prosperity. It is a
curious fact, however, that though, with a short interval,
cities of great importance existed at Hissarlik from about 2600
to 1184 B.C., the place was afterwards of no consequence, for
the three later settlements, the seventh, eighth, and ninth, were
relatively humble places.

FIG. 49. The site of Troy to-day.

The Second 'City' of Hissarlik was in reality a strong castle
or fort, defended by a steep ramp of small stones, roughly hewn
and laid together in mud, above which were vertical walls of
unburnt clay. The wall was pierced in two places by strongly
fortified gateways, and the space within the walls was scarcely
more than a hundred yards in diameter. During the long period
of the existence of this fortress, it had been twice rebuilt, and
the foundations of three successive walls have been laid bare
throughout almost the whole of their length.

Within the walls were a number of houses, of the megaron
or porched house type, examples of which we have already met

with at Erösd and Dhimini. We have seen, in an earlier chapter, reason for believing that the megaron was introduced into Dhimini and other sites in Thessaly from the Black Earth region of South Russia, and we cannot help feeling that some

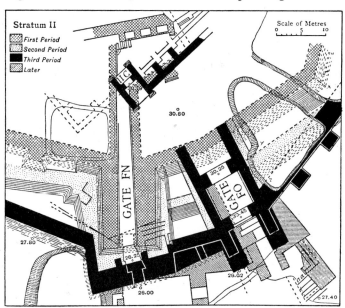

Fig. 50. The south gate of Hissarlik II. Third period.

influences from that region had reached Hissarlik. On the other hand, the characteristic painted pottery of that region is not found on the Asiatic site, where the vases are, for the most part, developments of the wares found in the first settlement. There seems to be some reason, however, for connecting the rise of the Second City of Hissarlik with those disturbances on the Russian steppe that we have described in our earlier chapters.

An important object, found in Hissarlik II, tends on the

whole to strengthen this surmise. We have seen that perforated stone axe-hammers are an important feature of the culture of parts of South Russia, and we are inclined to agree with Myres, Childe, and others that they spread thence to the Baltic region, as well as to Brittany and the British Isles and to parts both of France and Italy. We have suggested that they were copies in stone of metal weapons made in much earlier times in Mesopotamia; axes, somewhat of this type, with perforated sockets to hold the handles, have been found in several cemeteries in that country, while many in copper and some in a mixture of gold, silver, and copper with a trace of tin, were discovered early in 1927 at Ur, in graves lying many feet below remains of the first dynasty of that city. Some metal axe-hammers and axe-adzes, which remind us of the Mesopotamian models, have been found in South Russia.

Now the stone axe-hammers found in Hissarlik II include a remarkable set, made in beautiful stone and, one of them in particular, richly ornamented. The wooden shaft had apparently been surmounted by a finely worked knob of rock crystal. It is, therefore, very likely that these splendid objects had been insignia of authority; if so, it seems probable that the rulers of Hissarlik II had some connexion with the nomad people of the Russian steppe, whose intrusion into the Danube basin we have already described. It appears, however, that all such axe-hammers belong to the third phase of the Second City.

It seems likely, then, that the Second City of Hissarlik arose during the period of general disturbance described in previous chapters, and that conquerors from the Russian steppe passed down into Hissarlik, making themselves masters over the people of that region; it is also possible that they did the same at Dhimini and other fortified sites of the second period in Thessaly.

Hissarlik lay sufficiently near to the Aegean to enable its inhabitants to receive influences from the sea-folk of Crete and

the Cyclades, who could creep up the island-studded coast of
Asia Minor, even if they could not face the Etesian winds of the
more open sea. It is more than probable that the early mariners
found it difficult to work up against the perennially out-flowing
current of the Dardanelles and would require to take this part
of the voyage in easy stages; as soon as the seafarers from the
Aegean became interested in trading ventures with the coasts
of the Black Sea, such a post as Hissarlik, close to the narrow
sea-way, would gain in importance. Nevertheless there are
few objects of definitely Aegean workmanship among the re-

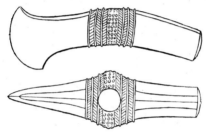

FIG. 51. Battle-axe from Treasure L. No. 1 of Hissarlik II.

mains discovered on that site. It is true that certain figurines
have been found there as well as pots with high spouts, which
remind us of those occurring in Crete and the Cyclades; these
may, however, be native to some part of Asia Minor, whence
they reached all three sites independently. Some of the daggers
from Hissarlik are, nevertheless, very like those discovered in
the Cyclades, where pots resembling those of Hissarlik II have
come to light. It seems probable, too, that the obsidian found
at this site came from Melos.

There are close connexions between Hissarlik II and the
Danube basin. We have already, in the preceding volume of
this series, noted resemblances between the wares of Hissarlik I
and some found at Vinča near Belgrade; these resemblances

seem to indicate that trade relations existed before the rise of the Second City. During the period under review these signs of commercial relations became more marked.

Professor Childe has shown us that two-handled vases, clearly imitated from metal originals from Hissarlik II, have been found in Hungary along the banks of the Danube and the Tisza, and even as far off as Silesia and Thuringia. Cypriote daggers, which almost certainly passed through Hissarlik II on

FIG. 52. Vases from Hissarlik II.

the way, have turned up at Csorvas near Arad in Transylvania, double-spiral ornaments made of copper wire, such as were found in Hissarlik II, occur at many sites in Hungary, while coiled ear-rings, another Hissarlik feature, have been found in Bohemia. Near Prague three mugs were found which might actually have come from Hissarlik II itself.

All this betokens a line of trade from Hissarlik to Hungary and thence to Bohemia, Silesia, and beyond. But traders do not carry their wares to poor peasant villages without some hope of reward. We have already seen that in the south-eastern section of the Hungarian Plain the peasants had been working gold and copper mines, and it is worth remembering in this connexion that both copper and tin are to be found in the Erzgebirge

between Bohemia and Saxony. It seems to us very likely that
Childe's suggestion is correct, and that the traders of Hissarlik
II had penetrated to the north of Bohemia in search of these
ores. This receives support from the fact that the first implements known to have been made of true bronze, with about
10 per cent. of tin, were found by Schliemann among the ruins

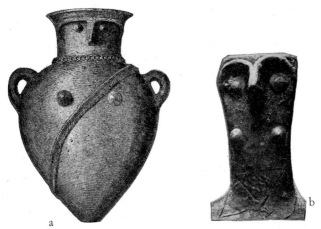

a

b

Fig. 53. Face-decorated wares: (a) Hissarlik II; (b) Cemetery A at Kish.

of the Second City, and seem to have belonged to its third or
latest phase.

Thus, although this settlement owed much of its prosperity
to its position near the south shore of the Dardanelles, a position that linked it with the maritime trade both of the Aegean
and the Black Seas, it had another and still more important
geographical advantage. It lay on what was at that early time
the best route from Asia Minor to Thrace and thence to the
metal-bearing regions of the Danube basin and the Erzgebirge.
Its curious pottery with face decorations reminds us of the
face-decorated handles of pots from Cemetery A at Kish in

Mesopotamia, though the latter were earlier by some centuries. Its red ware, coloured with red iron oxide, its high-spouted jugs, its pots with three legs, and the great majority of its daggers, are all suggestive of links across Asia Minor with Cyprus and Mesopotamia. At an early stage in the discussion that took place about the civilization of Hissarlik II, Myres emphasized very ably the debt that it owed to the sources from which Cyprus derived its early inspirations. All that has been discovered tends to show the importance of factors from Asia Minor and Mesopotamia, and to mark how these influences were carried across the straits to Thrace and the Danube basin.

Brooks and Ellsworth Huntington have both suggested that drought was the chief factor that caused disturbances on the steppe lands, bringing desolation upon the ancient civilizations of the river valleys and the Black Earth lands in the middle of the third millennium before our era. With this we feel disposed to agree, though we think that the taming of the horse, and the use of this animal as a companion in war, played a not inconsiderable part. It seems reasonable to suppose that these disturbances on land prompted men to an increased use of the sea.

That the untutored men of the steppe took kindly to the civilization that they had at first destroyed seems clear from evidence that we shall cite in the next volume of this series. This is specially true in Mesopotamia, where the destruction was not so complete and where the invaders seem to have had, before their arrival, some appreciation of the value of a settled state. The invaders in most cases became the rulers and the aristocracy of the civilized land that they had conquered, and in some cases brought to the old civilizations a vigorous and adventurous spirit that had before been lacking. This led to a fresh and more extensive expansion of trade, thus carrying the elements of civilization to the very bounds of Europe.

In this connexion it may not be amiss to think of the Norse

rovers, who only a thousand years ago were spreading southwards from their northern home, at first carrying destruction in their train, but afterwards establishing kingdoms and duchies from Britain to the Mediterranean Sea. These hardy Norsemen quickly acquired and assimilated the developed culture of the peoples they conquered, and ultimately helped to carry out the great adventure for the reconquest of the Holy Sepulchre. We are inclined to attribute the great and far-reaching activities of Hissarlik II, especially during its later stages, to some such leadership.

BOOKS

Schliemann, H. *Troy.*
Schliemann, H. *Ilium.*
Leaf, W. *Homer and History* (London, 1915).
Leaf, W. *Troy, a study in Homeric geography* (London, 1912).
Childe, V. Gordon. *The Dawn of European Civilization* (London, 1925).

9

Crete

WE have seen in a previous volume of this series, *Peasants and Potters*, that Sir Arthur Evans found at Knossos a deposit, eight metres in thickness, containing pottery, ground stone implements, but no metal. The absence of metal from such a large deposit suggests that it was unknown or at any rate scarce at that time. From a similar deposit at Phaestos, five metres in thickness, Mosso obtained the same kind of material, and an unworked piece of ivory from the tusk of an African elephant; this is another indication of connexions with Africa at that early date. We are thus justified in assuming that for many centuries the inhabitants of central Crete made pottery, while using only stone implements; towards the end of this neolithic phase we find evidence of connexions with Egypt, and a flat axe of copper has been found in a layer that seems to belong to the very close of this period.

As explained in the preceding volume of this series, *Priests and Kings*, Evans has devised a chronological scheme for the Early Metal Age in Crete. He has divided it into three great periods, which he has termed Early, Middle, and Late Minoan, and each of these into three phases, First, Second, and Third. Early Minoan I is a convenient term for the period of transition from the Neolithic Age mentioned in the last paragraph to the

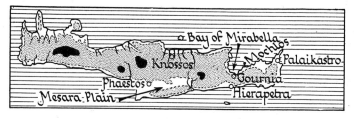

FIG. 54. Map of Crete.

remarkable developments of Early Minoan II, which we must now discuss.

Though a large number of ancient sites have been discovered in Crete and already excavated, we cannot be sure that we yet know even the majority of them, but judging by the evidence at present available it seems justifiable to believe that Knossos did not become a place of first importance until the beginning of the Middle Minoan period, and that during the Early Minoan period the principal activities were confined to the eastern end of the island, though we have evidence that a considerable population was occupying the Mesara Plain in the south. We must not forget, however, that it is possible that some of the Early Minoan layers at Knossos were cleared away to level the site for the Middle Minoan palace that arose there.

At the extreme eastern end of Crete we have the early site at Palaikastro, while a little to the west, off the north coast, lies the island of Mochlos. On the isthmus of Hierapetra, leading from east to central Crete, lies Vasiliki, another early site;

FIG. 55. Pottery of the Second Early Minoan period.

while Gournia, a fourth site, lies north of it, near the coast and at no great distance from Mochlos.

The little island of Mochlos lies in the bay of Mirabella, towards the eastern end of the north coast of Crete, and its very position suggests connexions with the mainland of Asia Minor as well as with the Cyclades; these connexions are confirmed by a study of the remains found there. On this island in 1908 Mr. Richard B. Seager found a large number of tombs, mostly dating from the second and third phases of the Early Minoan period. The form of the tombs, of which there were several types having interesting analogues elsewhere, will be discussed towards the end of this chapter; here we must confine our attention to their contents. Certain stone vases found in these tombs, with pottery of the type recognized as Early Minoan II, resemble forms used in Egypt during the Sixth Dynasty, as do certain. button seals. It has been concluded, therefore, that the Second Early Minoan phase, which is

FIG. 56. Stone bowl from Mochlos.

believed to have started about 2800 B.C., came to an end about or rather before 2400 B.C. Then followed the Third Early Minoan phase, which gave way to the First phase of the Middle Minoan period about 2200 or 2100 B.C., when settled government was again being established in Egypt under the Eleventh Dynasty.

The pottery of the Second Early Minoan phase is of various types. Some dark burnished wares show affinity to the previous style, though new shapes came into use; the best are decorated with geometrical patterns in dark paint on a light ground. Later on in this phase a curious mottled ware, found earlier on the neighbouring site of Vasiliki, came into more general use at Mochlos. During the Third Early Minoan phase the pottery became less frequently painted and sometimes incised decoration reappears; this has been thought to have been due to Cycladic influence. Connexions with Egypt, which had been very numerous during the previous phase, almost ceased during Early Minoan III, for trade with that country was at a standstill owing to its disturbed condition.

That the people of eastern Crete were prosperous during the Second Early Minoan phase is clear from the number of

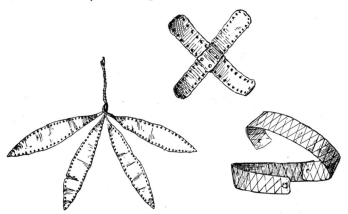

FIG. 57. Gold objects from Mochlos.

gold objects found in the tombs at Mochlos; the presence of a very fine set of jewellery in Tomb II, with pottery of this phase and one jug of early Minoan III type, suggests that the period of prosperity may have continued for a time after the connexions with Egypt had ceased. The gold work is of two types. One is repoussé work, the pattern being beaten out over a model bearing the design: in the other the patterns have been pressed through from behind with a pointed tool. The objects consist of diadems, pins, beads, and chains. The workmanship is, on the whole, primitive.

The tools used at this time consisted of copper knives or

daggers with a broad base; these are sometimes called triangular daggers. The form became somewhat longer and narrower at the base during the Third Early Minoan phase. Flat axes, somewhat triangular in form, are not uncommon, and there are tools closely resembling them. These have been called votive axes by Mosso, but Seager has shown that the handle was fixed vertically on to the end of the blade, and that they must have

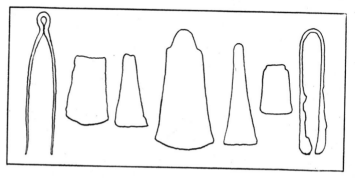

Fig. 58. Flat axes, cutters, and forceps from Mochlos.

been used as broad chisels or, as he calls them, cutters. Small depilatory forceps have also been found. At Mochlos Seager found one double axe of copper and two of lead, with holes perforated through the centre for the shaft. Dr. Chatzedakis found eighteen miniature specimens made of lead and one made of silver in the cave near the village of Arkalochori. The presence of these double axes seems to point to connexions with Caria on the mainland of Asia Minor and ultimately with Mesopotamia. The miniature specimens tell us that already in Early Minoan times the double axe had become, not only a symbol of authority, but a cult object.

It is usually believed that all the tools used during these two Early Minoan phases were of copper, and that bronze was then

unknown, though the contrary opinion has been expressed.
Many of the broad-based triangular daggers have been analysed,
and all thus treated have been found to be of pure copper.
Fragments of two of the longer and narrower daggers found in
a *tholos* or corbelled bee-hive tomb at Platanus on the Mesara
Plain have also been analysed. One of these was of pure copper,
while the other contained nearly two per cent. of tin. This

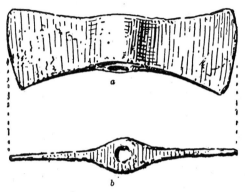

FIG. 59. Double axe from Mochlos.

possibly is only an accidental impurity and the dagger may be
attributed to the Third Early Minoan phase, since the presence
of a few Middle Minoan objects shows that the tomb in which
it was found was still in use in that period. Until, therefore, a
greater number of analyses have been made of implements
whose limiting dates can be fixed with certainty, it would not
be safe to pronounce whether bronze was known to the people of
Crete during the Early Minoan period.

The *tholoi* of the Mesara Plain have already been described in
the preceding volume of this series, *Priests and Kings*. While
they came into use during the second Early Minoan period they
continued to be opened and re-used until well on in the Middle

Minoan times. They seem to have been family, tribal, or communal burial places.

The tombs at Mochlos consist of five types. Belonging to the first type are six great ossuaries or chamber tombs of large size, entered through doorways closed by stone slabs. They lie on a narrow ledge below great cliffs on the north-west face of the island, in an isolated spot, and from their rich contents it

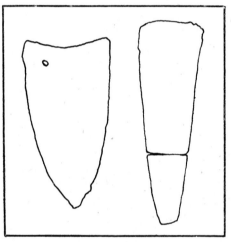

FIG. 60. Triangular and long daggers from Mochlos.

is supposed that they were the tombs of princely families. In some cases, at least, the tomb chamber is walled by the cliff on one side and by slabs or dry walling on the others; in others the cliff face itself is covered by slabs. The general plan is rectangular, apart from the irregularities of the cliff face. Evidence of a top is absent at present, but, as the doorways were carefully made and closed by great slabs, it seems likely that they were roofed. Seager has argued that there was probably a plastered roof over each, but that it fell in during Middle

Minoan times. Thus, when tomb-robbers came to rifle the
graves at the end of the Middle Minoan period, a quantity of
debris covered the treasures that had been laid there with the
Early Minoan dead. This circum-
stance probably saved a good deal
of the treasures for us, while the
tomb-robbers left various tell-tale
objects behind them.

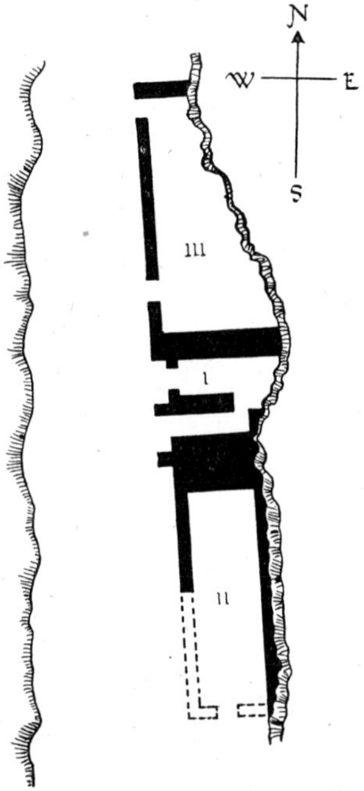

The second type consists of cist
graves, built of large thin upright
slabs, very much as in the early
graves in the Cycladic Islands.
The third type is very similar,
except that the walls consist partly
of upright slabs and partly of dry
walling of small stones. The fourth
type consists of graves placed in
holes in the rock; these are few in
number, and, judging by their
contents, the graves of poor per-
sons. Lastly, there was found a
small cave, containing a large mass
of bones and two pots.

The graves taken as a whole
seem to show a combination of
two types of tombs and methods

FIG. 61. Plans of chamber tombs
of Nos. I, II, and III at Mochlos.
(After Seager.)

of burial. Firstly, we have the
dry walling, as in the Mesara *tholoi*, but without the corbelling,
though this method of building is used in rare instances. Then
we have the cist of upright slabs occurring in the Cyclades. On
the other hand, the ossuary or family vault, unknown in the
Cyclades, but invariable on the Mesara Plain, is by far the most
important type.

From the foregoing descriptions we may gather that quite early in the Second Minoan phase, or perhaps considerably earlier, a group of traders arrived in the eastern part of Crete; the leaders seem to have settled in the island of Mochlos, though settlements were made elsewhere on the coast of the north-eastern corner of the island. The tombs of these people show Cycladic affinities, but since, as we have shown in the previous volume of this series, the population in the Cyclades seems to

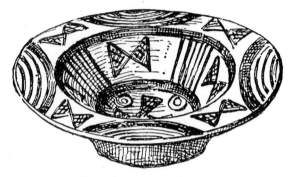

Fig. 62. Saucer of Syrian type.

have come from Caria, it is possible that these new arrivals in Crete came, not so much from the islands, as from the south-western corner of Asia Minor. Various other features in the culture both of eastern Crete and of the Cyclades, especially the presence of the double axe, seem to point to this conclusion.

The new-comers seem quickly to have adopted Cretan customs, especially the habit of using an ossuary. They carried on a brisk trade with other lands, but more particularly with the valley of the Nile, whence they imported bowls of stone. That they traded with other lands is also clear from the wealth of gold objects found in some of their tombs.

With the downfall of the Old Kingdom in Egypt, and the

ruin that overtook that land, the most profitable part of the trade of these eastern Cretan merchants came to an abrupt end, and with it the prosperity that they had enjoyed for some centuries. They were, however, not to be daunted. Though their old markets on the mainland, in Egypt and elsewhere, had been ruined by the irruption of nomads from the steppes, they turned their attention elsewhere; a saucer of Syrian type, found in a tomb at Mochlos, seems to indicate trade with that region or with Cyprus. As we shall see in the next chapter, they sought out fresh sources of the raw materials that they needed and fresh markets for their products, in the hitherto unexplored islands and peninsulas of the west.

BOOKS

Cambridge Ancient History, vol. i (Cambridge, 1923).

SEAGER, R. B. *Explorations in the Island of Mochlos* (Boston, 1912).

EVANS, SIR A. J. *The Palace of Minos at Knossos*, vol. i (London, 1921).

CHILDE, V. GORDON. *The Dawn of European Civilization* (London, 1925).

GLOTZ, G. *Aegean Civilization* (London, 1925).

XANTHOUDIDES, S. *The Vaulted Tombs of Mesara*. (Transl. by J. P. Droop) (London, 1924).

10

Maritime Trade

THE previous chapters have indicated the extent to which the peoples of Hissarlik II and their contemporaries in the Cyclades, and Crete, followed maritime pursuits. They fished, and searched the neighbouring lands for obsidian and other useful stone, and in due course for copper, tin, gold, and materials for ornaments. Life in the Aegean was sharply contrasted with life in Mesopotamia and Egypt. In the two latter countries efforts were made, occasionally with success, to give a unitary organization to a large area; in the Aegean, however, separation was the rule and diverse communities developed their traditions side by side, holding intercourse with one another without losing individuality. This state of affairs is natural enough in a region of islands and peninsulas, with ships as the chief means of communication.

A good deal of the maritime trade was at first rather 'hand to hand' than under the control of organized carriers with stations spread over long distances. Thus the evidence for this intercourse is chiefly the overlap of cultural provinces, especially illustrated by the distribution of portable objects. Idols, or figurines, mostly female, occur in Asia Minor, South Russia, East Central Europe, Thessaly, Hissarlik, the Cyclades, and Crete; and also, it would seem, in North Africa; from the last-named region, it has been suggested, came the idea of those figurines with enormously developed thighs which occur in Malta, Crete, and the Cyclades. Others, however, claim that all these figurines, representing as they do the Great Mother, indicate the presence of a cult that originated in Asia Minor. The special centre of distribution of these figurines seems to have been the Cyclades, whence they were carried to South Russia.

High-handled cups, apparently copied in pottery from metal models, are found at Hissarlik as well as in Thessaly and in the Danube basin; one fine example is known from Mochlos in Crete, but the idea seems foreign to that island. This form of cup, with decoration that seems to be of Thessalian origin, occurs in Sicily, and is one of the grounds on which Peet has suggested a trade-route between North Greece and South Italy and Sicily, probably across the Straits of Otranto, since examples of this type are known from the Terre d'Otranto. If this route were in existence, it may have been in some sense a barrier to the expansion of the maritime activity of the Aegean peoples up the Adriatic Sea.

To return to the distribution of cultural elements, we may

FIG. 63. High-handled cups from (a) Sicily, (b) Thessaly, (c) Hissarlik.

next note pots or jugs with a long upward-pointing spout, called by the German archaeologists *Schnabelkannen*. These occur in Cyprus, at Hissarlik and at Yortan, and in the Cyclades; a few were met with at Mochlos, more on the Mesara Plain, while they have been found in Sardinia and one, it is said, in Sicily. Pots shaped like hour-glasses, again, occur at Hissarlik II, in the Cyclades, and occasionally in Crete. They have been found, too, in Thessaly and Central Greece, as well as in Galicia; also in Sicily and in the Arena Candida cave in Liguria. Basins on a high foot are known from Predynastic Egypt, Mesopotamia, Hissarlik, the Cyclades, and Crete; they have also been found in Sicily, Spain, and the Baltic region, as well as in Central Europe and at Butmir in Bosnia. Pots shaped like a modern sauce-boat are a marked feature in the early layers in Crete, as well as in Central Greece; they occur also in Sicily, Spain, France, and in the cave of Arena Candida in Liguria. Twin and triplet vessels are known from Egypt, Hissarlik, the Cyclades, Ruthenian Galicia, Italy, Spain, Eastern France, and Ireland.

These examples suffice to demonstrate that the Aegean peoples had relations with Sicily, South Italy, and the coasts and islands of the Western Mediterranean; the connexions with these last were, in all probability, to some extent indirect, whereas those with Sicily and perhaps with Sardinia were fairly direct and intimate, as we shall see later when we discuss the graves of these regions. Tombs of the Aegean type spread westward with this intercourse in a most marked fashion; this suggests that Cycladic relations were especially close with Sicily, but whether they reached this island entirely by sea, or across Greece, or both, is a matter that requires discussion. It seems as if the trade-routes from Hissarlik limited to a considerable extent the Cycladic activities to the north, and we get a general impression of different routes being in the hands of various groups of traders, barring one another out and, perhaps,

a

b

c

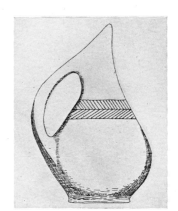

d

Fig. 64. Schnabelkannen from (a) Cyprus, (b) Hissarlik, (c) Cyclades, (d) Sardinia.

keeping the details of their own routes as secret as possible. Nevertheless, there was some general exchange of goods, and we are inclined to recognize, for example, Cycladic influences in South Russia.

The evidence gained from the distribution of different types of tombs is most instructive. In most of the Isles of the Cyclades have been found graves, each holding a single interment; these

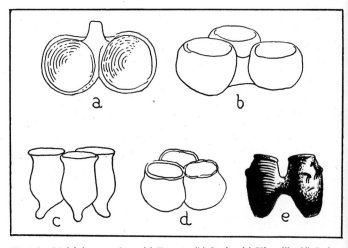

Fig. 65. Multiple vases from (a) France, (b) Spain, (c) Hissarlik, (d) Italy, (e) Egypt.

have been found at Pelos in the island of Melos, Paros, Antiparos, Naxos, Amorgos, and Siphnos. These graves, which date back into very early Cycladic times, are lined with flat slabs of local rock, rarely exceeding a metre in their greatest dimension. In the north-west of Syros island interments, mostly individual, are in tombs, the sides of which are all built of dry walling, sometimes slightly corbelled at the top, and covered with large slabs; sometimes these are built of very large stones, and they are usually provided with a porch. The use of upright slabs of local rock in the construction of tombs is the important factor in these tombs. In the island of Euboea, just beyond the Cycladic group, the tombs seem to have been excavated in

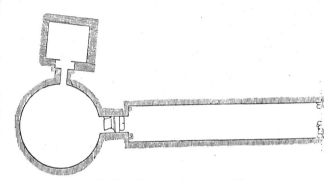

Fig. 66. The Treasury of Atreus at Mycenae.

the rock; this, as we have seen, occurred, though rarely, at Mochlos, and this style was adopted, in rather later time, in the neighbourhood of Knossos.

On the other hand, on the Mesara Plain, in the south of Crete, we have circular *tholoi* or bee-hive tombs of dry walling, corbelled in the upper part till the walls nearly meet, and covered finally with a slab. The entrance to these tombs was a low doorway, with upright stones for jambs and a large stone for a lintel. Outside the doorway, which was closed with a large slab, was a rectangular court enclosed by a low dry wall. These tombs, which seem to have been built on the plan of the early Libyan houses, were of the nature of ossuaries and were used from time to time for fresh interments through the course of several centuries. Such *tholoi* were at a later date erected in most parts of Crete and reach their most complete form later in the so-called Treasury of Atreus at Mycenae.

The resemblance between these *tholoi* and the Libyan houses was first pointed out by Sir Arthur Evans; Oric Bates found very similar tombs in Eastern Libya, and tombs of a like form, belonging to Libyan peoples, in Nubia and in the desert east of Hieraconpolis on the Nile. Some tombs and sepulchral circles of a much later date, found by Randall MacIver and Wilkins in South-western Algeria, seem to have features in common with these. Bates also found what seemed to be the lower portions of domed vaults on Seal Island, in the Gulf of Bombah, known to the Greeks as Plataea, on the African coast just opposite to the southern promontory of Crete. It would seem, then, that the tomb of corbelled dry walling linked with the custom of using ossuaries came from Libya, though we must remember that neither custom obtained on the Nile, except intrusively from the desert. Corbelling has been found by Woolley at Ur of the Chaldees, but there it was not associated with any idea of an ossuary.

At Mochlos, as we have seen, the majority of the tombs were built in the Cycladic style with upright slabs, though a certain amount of dry walling was used, as was also the practice in Syros. These tombs are, however, much larger than those in the Cyclades, the doorways were at one end and were closed with a large slab, as in the Mesara *tholoi*, while, like the latter, they were used for a succession of burials. At Mochlos, where we

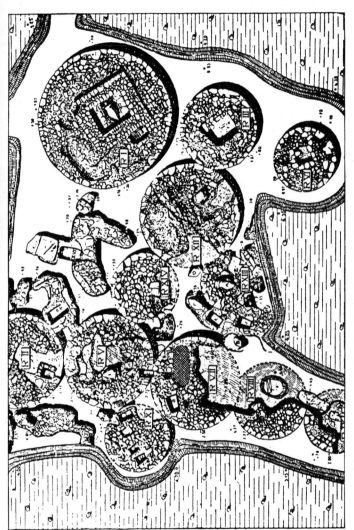

FIG. 67. Tombs in the island of Leukas.

seem to have a settlement of Cycladic traders upon Cretan soil, we have a curious mixture of the architecture and burial customs of Crete and the Cyclades.

We may, therefore, take it that the burial customs of Crete contained elements derived from Libya as well as from the Cyclades, and that the latter had almost certainly come from the south-west corner of Asia Minor. Unfortunately, we know little or nothing of the early graves in Thessaly; in the Peloponnese there are rock-cut tombs, each containing a number of burials, and on the island of Leukas or Levkas, which lies in the Adriatic Sea near the mouth of the Gulf of Corinth, is a collection of cists like those in the Cyclades, but surrounded by a circle of stones. Thus the principle of multiple burial was used on the mainland of Greece as well as in Crete, while the pottery there shows links both with the Cyclades and Hissarlik.

In Sicily we find that the earliest burials of the age with which we are dealing were in caves, and with the bodies was placed pottery, well made but of a rather coarse-grained clay; with a burial of this period in a cave at Villafrati near Palermo was found a 'Bell Beaker', a type of pot about which much will be said in a later volume. For the present it is sufficient to say that this type of pot occurs also in Sardinia and was a conspicuous feature in the Iberian peninsula when metal was just coming into use in that region. In another cave, at no great distance from the former, some painted pottery was found; this suggests the arrival of Aegean influences, for from the very beginning of the Metal Age painted pottery was in use in Crete, Thessaly, and the Black Earth region. A cave burial in the Grotta San Lazzaro, in the south-east of the island, contained human bones and those of animals, a few stone implements, and pottery, some of which was painted.

Of apparently slightly later date are many rock-cut tombs in several districts of Sicily, as well as burials in caves. The rock-cut tombs are usually entered through a short passage or *dromos* and the chambers sometimes contained a number of skeletons, deposited in special postures, after the flesh had been removed. This type of tomb is clearly akin to those of Leukas and to those

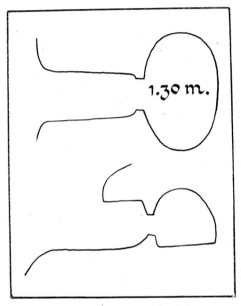

Fig. 68. Rock-cut tomb in Sicily.

of continental Greece already mentioned. Other tombs are smaller, though still larger than those of the Cyclades; they also show evidence of numerous burials. At Monte Racello, in the south-east of Sicily, have been found cave burials, rock-cut tombs, and tombs built up by setting together large slabs of rock; here, too, there are numerous burials in the same tomb. One tomb at Monte Racello, built up so as to leave a window at one end, has been compared by many archaeologists with the dolmens of the West, which will be described in the next volume of this series.

It is well to remember at this stage that the ideas of collective burial, and of ossuaries, which are not quite the same thing, seem to be specially characteristic of Crete, the latter having come from Libya. There are no corbelled tombs in Sicily, and this may be thought to weaken the argument we have been

Fig. 69. Figurines of fat women from Hal Saflieni, Malta.

advancing; on the other hand, in the soft limestone of south-east Sicily rock-cutting is an easy and attractive form of tomb construction, and, since some of the Sicilian tombs have vaulted roofs, that feature may be reminiscent of the corbelling of the Mesara *tholoi*. We must remember, too, that there was no corbelling at Mochlos, and we cannot yet say which Cretan group may have influenced the mainland of Greece, Leukas, and Sicily during the early times with which we are dealing. Mochlos was in close touch with the Cyclades, and Cycladic features are characteristic of these early Sicilian tombs.

In Malta there are dolmens and great sanctuaries of megalithic type, which will be described in the next volume, as well
as the great hypogeum of Hal Saflieni. The figurines found here
link Malta to the Cyclades and Crete, while the spiral decoration
resembles that found in Sicily. In Sardinia there are rock-cut
tombs, approached by a corridor; these contain numerous

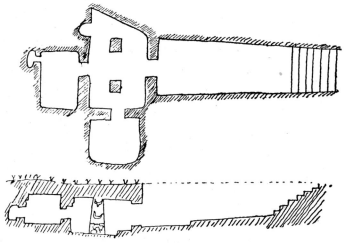

FIG. 70. Megalithic tomb at Anghelu Ruju.

chambers with stone-blocked doors. These chambers have, in
some cases, yielded remains of several individuals, and the tombs
sometimes have the chambers on either side of a corridor.
There are also cave burials in the island and other types of
tombs, a description of which must be left to the next volume.

In the Balearic Islands there are *naus* or *navetas*, which are
usually rock-cut tombs with lateral chambers in some cases.
The roofs may be built up by corbelling in some cases; in others
they are covered by flat slabs of stone. Hemp thinks that the
Grotte-des-Fées, near Arles, long thought to be a passage

dolmen, is really a rock-cut tomb, related to, but not identical with, those of the Balearics. This seems to us to be probable, but the relation of walls to roof reminds us of some Sicilian tombs. Corridor tombs, cut in the solid rock, with trench-like entrances lined with slabs, are also well known in the valley of

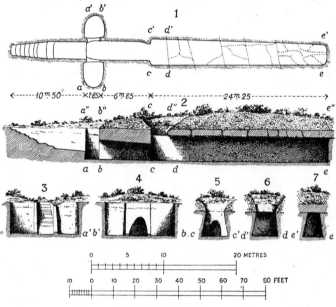

FIG. 71. The Grotte-des-Fées, near Arles.

the Marne in France. There is thus every indication of the extension of the rock-cut tomb westward in Mediterranean lands, and of its modification in the direction of a corridor plan with a trench-like entrance. In the next volume we shall have occasion to discuss the spread of the art of corbelling to the Iberian peninsula and beyond.

It is thus obvious, both from the nature of the objects found

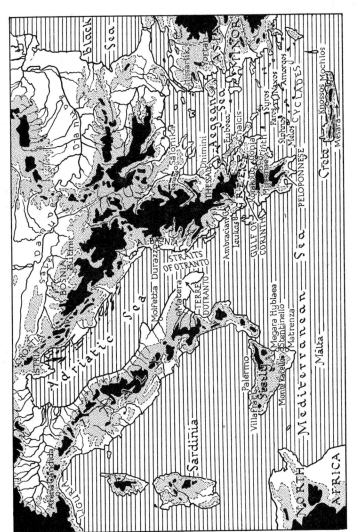

Fig. 72. Map of the trade-routes in the Mediterranean.

and the forms of the tombs, that connexions between the eastern and western ends of the Mediterranean Sea were developed during Early Minoan times, when metal was first reaching the West. Several of the objects found in the West have been shown to belong to one or other of the civilizations of Hissarlik, Crete, or the Cyclades; thus there remains no shadow of a doubt that these influences were carried from East to West.

In considering the transmission of these elements of culture, we must look upon Sicily as in some respects the most westerly out-post of the eastern region; nevertheless, it was the base from which these influences reached more westerly lands. It was, in fact, a junction of routes of intercourse, leading to the East, the North, and the West. We must be careful, however, not to assume that the culture of Western Europe was derived wholesale from the Eastern Mediterranean; certain elements, such as the knowledge of metallurgy and probably the potter's art, seem to have been introduced, and these with other factors served to stimulate the people of the West to develop their own independent civilization.

Quite recently Dr. H. Frankfort has made some interesting suggestions as to the trade-routes in use through the eastern half of the Mediterranean at this time. He notes that there have been found in the Istrian Peninsula, at the head of the Adriatic Sea, fragments of pottery which have been influenced by the wares of Hissarlik II. He suggests that the trade-route, which passed, as we have shown, from Hissarlik to Bohemia and beyond, branched also up the Save Valley, turning southwards to Butmir, but also following the Save westward and thence through Croatia to the head of the Adriatic.

He has pointed out, too, that there was trade between Hissarlik and some early settlements of Cycladic origin on the coasts of the island of Euboea, especially in the neighbourhood of Chalcis. He makes a further suggestion that there was another trade-route from Hissarlik to the Adriatic, though he admits

that no positive evidence for this is available. Such a route
would have presented great difficulties. If it started from
Chalcis it could have passed up the Spercheios Valley to its head,
but it would then have encountered wild and very mountainous
country before reaching the Ambracian Gulf just north of

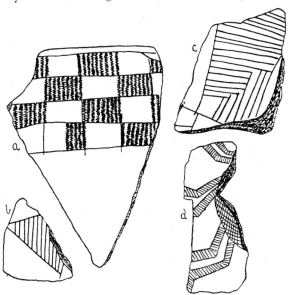

Fig. 73. Fragments of incised ware from Matera.

Leukas. A better, but still difficult, land route would have been
from Salonika, by what was afterwards known as the Via
Egnatia, to Durazzo in Albania.

Frankfort has pointed out that Cycladic folk from Argolis
settled not only at Corinth but also in a number of villages in
that neighbourhood, one of which was actually on the isthmus.
These villages had already a somewhat mixed population, for,
though actually founded by the first Thessalian folk, some of

the people responsible for the Dhimini pottery, people who hailed originally from the Black Earth lands, were settled at Gonia, one of these villages, while emigrants from Hungary, bringing First Danubian pottery, had taken refuge at Korakou, another of the same group. Into this mixed population came the Cycladic traders with their characteristic *Urfirnis*, or primitive glazed pottery.

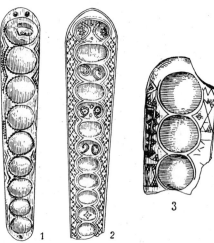

FIG. 74. Knobbed bone objects from (1) Hissarlik and (2, 3) Sicily.

From the neighbourhood of Corinth these traders, carrying with them elements from the other civilizations of that neighbourhood, sailed, he thinks, down the Gulf of Corinth and made settlements in Leukas, for in the cave of Chirospilia in that island have been found fragments of the pottery used by all these people. Here, he believes, they were joined by others who had sailed down from the head of the Adriatic Sea, and perhaps by traders who had come more directly from Hissarlik by the trans-peninsular route that he has postulated.

From Leukas some of the traders crossed the Adriatic, for evidence of their influence has been found in pottery discovered at Matera and Molfetta on the coast of Italy. Others again skirted the south shore of Italy and made settlements in the south-east of Sicily. Here they found humble villages, such as those of Stentinello and Matrenza, inhabited by fisher-folk, who used well-made pottery decorated with incised designs but were ignorant of metal. Such civilization as these people possessed seems to have come from North Africa. The settlements were clearly not all made by the same traders, for pottery, reminding us of Dhimini ware, occurs at Megara Hyblaea, while at other places we have rock-cut tombs resembling those in Euboea, and various objects which occur also in Hissarlik. From Sicily traders occasionally called at Malta, where they found a neolithic civilization, probably of African origin, and more frequently in Sardinia, whence trade passed to the west and to the north-east.

It is difficult to give any precise dates for this trade. The presence of wares, derived from those of Dhimini at such sites as Gonia, Leukas, Molfetta, and Megara Hyblaea, indicates that this trade cannot have begun until well after the beginning of the Second Thessalian period. The curious knobbed bone object found in Sicily belongs to the second phase of Hissarlik II, which we must equate roughly with the Third Early Cycladic phase, between 2400 and 2000 B.C. We may be reasonably certain, therefore, that this western extension of Aegean trade was being carried on during this period and we have no certain evidence that it had begun earlier.

BOOKS

CHILDE, V. GORDON. *The Dawn of European Civilization* (London, 1925).
PEET, T. ERIC. *The Stone and Bronze Ages in Italy* (Oxford, 1909).
FRANKFORT, H. *Studies in the Early Pottery of the Near East*, vol. ii (London, 1927).

II

The Last Days of Sumer

IN the preceding volume we traced the fortunes of the kingdom of Agade to its close. During the later years of that
dynasty there had been constant trouble with the wild tribes
living in the mountain country to the north; these were known,
as we have stated in a previous chapter, as the people of Su and
Gu. The fall of the dynasty with the death of Gimil-dural in
2571 B.C. seems to have been due to these people, and for a time
the records in Akkad are silent. We can only assume that the
people of Gu, now known as Gutium, had conquered the land,
for the Scheil dynastic table ends with the words: 'The royalty
was taken to the hosts of Gutium which had no kings', and the
Weld-Blundell prism asks the significant questions: 'Who was
king ? Who was not king ?'

Although Akkad had fallen to the invaders, the southern
cities of Sumer for a time kept their independence. Under the
leadership of Erech they held out for thirty years, but no contemporary documents of this period have yet been found. We
only know from the dynastic lists that five kings reigned
successively at Erech, forming the fourth dynasty of that city,
and that their rule came to an end in 2541 B.C. As the dynasty
of Gutium follows in the lists, it is clear that these northern
invaders had by this date gained control over the whole of
Mesopotamia and perhaps of still further portions of the empire
of Sargon.

These invaders were evidently barbarians, and for the period
of their dominance there is a singular lack of evidence. The
dynastic tables tell us that twenty-one kings ruled for 125 years
and forty days, and give some of the names of these kings. They

moved the seat of government to Arrapkha, which has been thought to have been at Kerkuk, east of Arbela, and thither they carried from Agade the statue of Anunit, another name for Ishtar, at once the queen of heaven and the goddess of battle, and doubtless spoils from other cities. A few fragments from Nippur and elsewhere contain lamentations over the calamities that had befallen the cities of Sumer and Akkad owing to the actions of these men of Gutium. One of the kings of this dynasty, Lasirab, who may be identified with the thirteenth given in the Weld-Blundell prism, where he appears as . . . . rabum, dedicated a stone mace-head to the temple at Sippar. A tablet, found at Nippur and containing a compilation of older inscriptions, mentions another king, E-irridupizir or Enrida-pizir, who seems to have been one of the last of the kings of this dynasty. At length the rule of these barbarians became in-tolerable, and, taking advantage of the accession of a weak monarch, Tiriga(n), sometimes called Tirikhan, Terikhan, or Tiriqan, Utukhegal of Umma raised a revolt against Gutium, which he described as 'the dragon of the mountain, enemy of the gods'. He defeated Tirigan after the latter had reigned but forty days, and pursued the defeated monarch to his fortress of Dubrum, where he was abandoned by his followers and taken prisoner with his wife and children.

Although there are few records relating to Mesopotamia as a whole during the rule of Gutium, we are not without informa-tion as to the fortunes of Lagash and Umma during this time, though we can date the events recorded with only approximate accuracy. During the reigns of some of the later kings of Agade, Ur-Bau was *patesi* of Lagash, where he erected or restored many temples. He had two daughters, Ningandu, who married Nammakhni, and another daughter who married Urgar; first Urgar and then Nammakhni became *patesi* of Lagash and the latter was succeeded by Ur-Ninsum.

Later than Ur-Bau, about 2500 B.C., there arose another *patesi* who became very distinguished. This was Gudea, whose statues, found at Telloh, are well known, and who was afterwards deified. He ruled as *patesi* for a long period, during which he was an enthusiastic builder of temples. Though he lived, there is no doubt, during the rule of the dynasty of Gutium, he makes no reference to these monarchs and, in spite of the disturbed state of the country, he was able to obtain gold from Melukhkha, which he said was in a mountain called Khakhu, silver from the 'silver mountains', which were in the Taurus range, and copper from Magda, which is said lay in the province of the city Rimash, and was probably somewhere in the Zagros range. He obtained porphyry from Melukhkha and marble from Tidanu, the Amorite mountain, presumably the Anti-Lebanon; he also obtained cedar from the Amanus range that lies between Syria and Cilicia.

At his death he was succeeded by his son Ur-Ningirsu, of whom nothing more is known. The figure of Gudea looms large in subsequent Sumerian literature. He was looked upon as the apostle of classical literature and the mysteries of the gods. After his death he was deified, and received libations of wine and meal at the feast of the new moon at Lagash. At Umma we have only the names of a few *patesis*, Lugal-annatum, Nammakhni, Galu-Babbar, and last of all Utukhegal, who, as we have seen, brought the rule of Gutium to an end.

After his victory Utukhegal moved the seat of his government to Erech, thus founding the fifth dynasty of that city. Some dynastic tables say that there were three kings of this dynasty, but the Weld-Blundell prism gives Utukhegal as the only monarch and attributes to him a reign of seven years. Nothing further is known of his doings and in 2409 B.C. he was succeeded by Ur-Engur, who founded the third dynasty of Ur.

Ur-Engur, sometimes called Ur-Nammu, Ur-id or Ur-

Lammu, soon established his rule over most of the wide territories formerly governed by Sargon. He rebuilt many temples in various cities and erected fine buildings in his capital. He adopted the title of 'King of Ur, King of Sumer and Akkad',

FIG. 75. Seated figure of Gudea.

and after a reign of eighteen years he died in 2391 B.C., when he was succeeded by Dungi his son.

Dungi seems to have extended his dominions in the east to include Elam and Anshan, and one of his daughters was married to the *patesi* of the latter state. In spite of that, Anshan revolted and was devastated by Dungi in 2347 B.C. A second

I 2

daughter of Dungi married the king of Markhashi, another Elamite province, near Awan, but this alliance was no more successful than the other in preserving peace, for the Elamite states were in a constant state of revolt during the closing years of Dungi's reign.

The extension of the dominions in the north-west was more

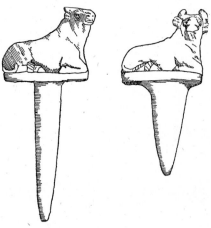

FIG. 76. Copper figures of bulls surmounting cones which were employed as votive offerings in the reigns of Gudea and Dungi.

successful. There seems little doubt that these reached to the Mediterranean coast of Syria, as had those of Sargon; and Langdon believes that this rule extended beyond the Taurus mountains into the heart of Asia Minor. At Kara-Euyuk, in the Halys valley, there was at an early date a settlement of Sumerians, and a vast number of clay tablets have been found there, containing records of their commercial transactions. Most of these date from a slightly later time, but the seal on one of them contains the following inscription: 'To the divine Ibi-Sin, mighty king, King of Ur, King of the four regions. Ur-Lugal-banda the scribe, son of Ur-nigingar thy servant'. Ibi-Sin was the last king of Ur, and the conditions of the kingdom during his reign make it unlikely that he had been responsible for this great extension of the dominions of that city. During the reign of Dungi the land was more prosperous than before or after, and he and his father, Ur-Engur, were the only two monarchs of this dynasty who are known to have made extensive conquests. It seems likely, therefore, that this Sumerian expansion into Cappadocia, leading to settlements in the Halys valley, and the exploitation of the copper mines of that part, must be placed at this time, if not earlier.

Dungi had a long reign, but his latter years were much troubled by revolts of Elamite tribes, some of which were put down with difficulty. At last, after a reign of forty-six or forty-seven years, he died in the year 2345 B.C., and was succeeded by his son Bur-Sin. This monarch had considerable trouble with the turbulent tribes living on the slopes of the Zagros mountains throughout the eight years of his reign. He seems to have been able to keep his empire intact, though there is no evidence that he extended its bounds. He died in 2337 B.C. and was succeeded by his son Gimil Sin, sometimes called Migir-Sin, a Semitic rendering of the Sumerian name Shu-Sin.

Like his father, Gimil-Sin had constant trouble with the tribes in the Zagros range, more particularly with those in the north, for the Elamite states farther south seem to have remained quiet. He also feared trouble in the north-west, the land of Amurru, and from Tidnu or Tidanu, which has been identified with the mountain region of the Anti-Lebanon. Against this danger he erected a wall, which was called the Amorite Wall 'Murek-Tidnim' or 'the Wall which keeps Tidnu at a distance'. It is not known where this wall was, but it has been suggested that it might have been between the two rivers near Sippar. It is clear that his power was becoming weak and that there was trouble on his borders, but he seems to have kept the Mesopotamian portion of his empire intact.

Gimil-Sin died in 2328 B.C. and was succeeded by his son Ibi-Sin, who spent his long reign of twenty-five years in attempting to avert the destruction of what was left to him of his empire. At first he was partially successful in subduing the desert tribes, some of which attacked him from the north and some from the south, but ultimately the Elamites, who had up till then remained submissive, revolted against his rule. In 2301 B.C. Kutur-nakhunte, King of Elam, combined with Ishbi-Girra, King of Maer, to attack him. Between them they destroyed the city of Ur and took possession of his kingdom.

Though some part of Mesopotamia thus came under the sway of the Elamites, the remainder passed to Ishbi-Girra, who established his capital at Isin. In the far north-west, however, the Amurru, as the steppe-folk of this region were then called, 'that never knew a city', were gradually organizing themselves into a power that was soon to be felt in Mesopotamia. One small Sumerian state seems to have retained its independence, for Larsa, or Ellasar, appears, for a time at least, to have remained independent of Isin and Elam.

Isin lay about fifty miles north of Ur, midway between the Tigris and the Euphrates, and at the fall of the kingdom of Ibi-Sin, Ishbi-Girra became its first king; at the same time Naplanum, who appears also to have come from the north-west, set up an independent kingdom at Larsa, a few miles farther south.

Four kings of his line succeeded Ishbi-Girra at Isin, and reigned until 2206 B.C., when the last of these, Lipit-Ashdar or Lipit-Ishtar, was expelled. A record says that he was driven out by the Amurru, but the king who succeeded, Ur-Ninurta, bore a Sumerian name, and it is surmised that he came to the throne as the result of a Sumerian revolt. Up to this time the

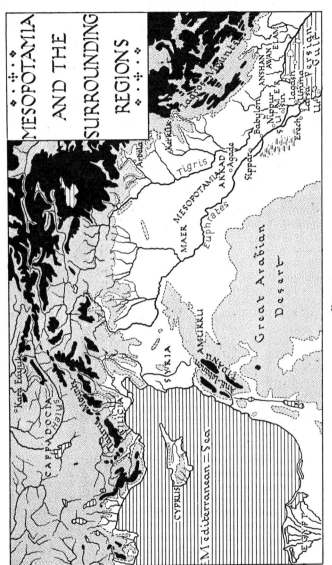

MESOPOTAMIA AND THE SURROUNDING REGIONS

FIG. 77.

relations between Isin and Larsa had been most amicable, but after the accession of Ur-Ninurta the two states were constantly at war, each endeavouring to wrest from the other the supremacy over Sumer and Akkad. Ur-Ninurta first marched against the people of Su, and in his desire to extend his kingdom southwards came into conflict with Gungunum, the fifth king of Larsa. Gungunum was, however, engaged in attacking Bashimi, which lay not far from Sippar, and later on attacked and defeated Anshan. Then, after a period of peace, he built a wall around Larsa, and about 2191 B.C. attacked one of the cities of Isin. Further trouble occurred between these two states about fourteen years later. These wars were, however, of short duration, being little more than raids on one another's lands after the harvest had been gathered in. Abi-sare succeeded his father Gungunum in 2181 B.C. and in 2178 B.C. Ur-Ninurta died and his rule passed to his son Bur-Sin. In the meantime the pressure from the south-west was growing. Finally in 2169 B.C. the Amurru broke through the wall by Sippar and took possession of the northern part of Akkad; they fixed their capital at Babylon, where Sumu-abu ascended the throne as the first monarch of the First Babylonian Dynasty.

In spite of constant threats and attacks from all sides, from the people of Su and Gu on the north, from the Elamites on the east and from the Amurru and other desert tribes on the west and south, some of the Sumerian cities contrived to maintain their civilization unimpaired. During the time that the dynasty of Gutium was in power the records are scanty and the cities that felt their rule were depressed. At Lagash, however, Gudea contrived to continue the good work of his predecessors, and this city seems to have escaped the misfortunes that befell its rivals. Here at any rate Sumerian learning and civilization was kept alive until, after the expulsion of the Gutium kings, it flourished again under Dungi. No striking change was wit-

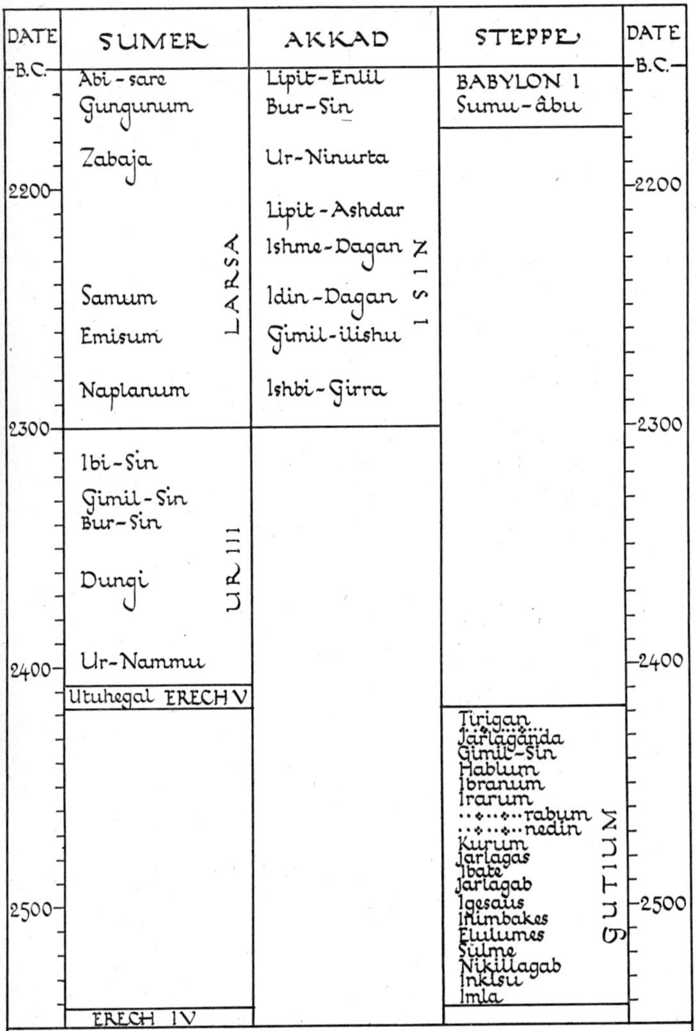

DATE B.C.	SUMER	AKKAD	STEPPE	DATE B.C.
	Abi-sare	Lipit-Enlil	BABYLON 1	
	Gungunum	Bur-Sin	Sumu-âbu	
	Zabaja	Ur-Ninurta		2200
2200		Lipit-Ashdar		
		Ishme-Dagan		
	Samum	Idin-Dagan		
	Emisum	Gimil-ilishu		
	Naplanum	Ishbi-Girra		
2300				2300
	Ibi-Sin			
	Gimil-Sin			
	Bur-Sin			
	Dungi			
	Ur-Nammu			2400
2400	Utuhegal ERECH V			
			Tirigan	
			Jarlaganda	
			Gimil-Sin	
			Hablum	
			Ibranum	
			Irarum	
			…◊…◊…rabum	
			…◊…◊…nedin	
			Kurum	
			Jarlagas	
			Ibate	
			Jarlagab	
			Igesaus	2500
2500			Inimbakes	
			Elulumes	
			Silme	
			Nikillagab	
			Inkisu	
			Imla	
	ERECH IV			

(Column labels within SUMER: LARSA, UR III; within AKKAD: NISIN; within STEPPE: GUTIUM)

Fig. 78 Chronological chart of kings of Mesopotamia

Note. The chart reads, in order of time, from the bottom upwards

nessed and civilization in the Mesopotamian cities seems to have stood still.

At this period a trading post established by Sumerians at Kara-Euyuk in the heart of Asia Minor possessed great importance. The extension of the dominions of a city by conquest had been effected in much earlier times, and it is to later days that we must look for the establishment of self-governing colonies at sea-ports on the coasts of undeveloped lands. The trading post at Kara-Euyuk cannot come under this head, for there is little doubt that the settlement was in the land of a rising power, of which we shall have more to say in later volumes, that of the Hatti, better known as the Hittites. A similar settlement was planted, more than a thousand years later, by the Greeks at Naucratis in Egypt. It seems possible, too, that Phoenician traders established similar communities in the trading cities of other people.

This settlement of the Sumerians at Kara-Euyuk is, however, the first instance that we have met with of a trading community living peaceably in the country of another people; it resembles most the communities of the Jews, found in almost every commercial city in the world to-day. In this connexion we may remember that Abraham set out from Ur of the Chaldees.

BOOKS

The Cambridge Ancient History, vol. i (Cambridge, 1923).

KING, L. W. *A History of Sumer and Akkad* (London, 1910).

12

Chaos in Egypt

THE great civilization of the Old Kingdom in Egypt dis-
appeared rapidly on the fall of the Sixth Dynasty. For several
generations the royal power had been failing, and additional
responsibilities had been laid on the great nobles or hereditary
princes as they were now styled. During the long reign of
Pepi II hill tribes from Judaea had been menacing the north-
eastern frontier, while negroes from the south had invaded
Nubia and threatened to enter Egypt. For some centuries after
the Sixth Dynasty had come to an end in 2475 B.C. the almost
complete lack of monuments shows us that the country was in
difficulties, and it is only from a few papyri, written perhaps
shortly after the troubles were past, but describing the calamities that had befallen the land, that we can get any information
as to what had happened.

A papyrus at Leningrad relates how pastoral tribes from
Palestine 'tried to come down to Egypt to beg for water after
their wont and to give drink to their flocks'. Another papyrus
at Leiden, translated under the title of 'The Admonitions of an
Egyptian Sage', states that 'a foreign tribe from abroad has
come to Egypt' and 'The Marsh-lands in their entirety are not
hidden. Lower Egypt can boast of trodden roads. The Asiatics
are skilled in the crafts of the Marsh-lands'; and again, 'The
tribes of the desert have become Egyptians everywhere', '(The
inhabitants) of the Marshes carry shields'.

Another document, attributed to the father of Merikara, a
king of the Ninth Dynasty, describes these invaders more
clearly. 'Behold the wretched Asiatic,' says the king, 'As for
him he can never abide in one place, his legs are ever in motion,
and he is always fighting since the days of Horus.'

From these statements we may conclude that the nomad pastoral tribes, which had attempted to cross into Egypt during the closing years of Pepi II, had at last succeeded, and had by degrees taken possession of the Delta. This is a repetition of what had happened, probably more than once, in predynastic days, and what happened again, in more organized fashion, on several later occasions. Moret believes that the unsettled condition of these tribes at this time was due to the movements of the Amurru, who were then advancing on Mesopotamia. To us it appears more likely that both movements were due to the same cause, the southward spread of the people of Asia Minor, who were later to be known as the Hittites. Whether these folk were already governed and led by Aryan chiefs from the Northern Steppe, as they were some centuries later, is at present uncertain.

Petrie believes that the Seventh and Eighth Dynasties, which ruled at Memphis, were the leaders of these Asiatics, though Breasted thinks that the Seventh Dynasty consisted of groups of nobles, and that the Eighth was composed of descendants of the monarchs of the Sixth. Later on, the power of the latter was disputed by another Dynasty, the Ninth, which arose at Heracleopolis in Middle Egypt, though the Eighth continued to rule at Memphis. Petrie believes that these were invaders from the Libyan desert, but most authorities see them in another line of nobles. Two Dynasties, the Ninth and Tenth, numbering between them at least eighteen kings, reigned at Heracleopolis, and came to an end about 2160 B.C.

It would seem that one of these kings of Heracleopolis attempted, not without some success, to drive out the Asiatics from the Delta, for the document attributed to the father of Merikara contains these statements: 'Since I have existed I have caused the Delta to crush the Asiatic, I have carried off captive the inhabitants (of their land), I have raided their flocks. The

Amu (Asiatic) is an abomination to Egypt. Still do not disquiet thyself on his account . . . he may indeed plunder an isolated encampment, but he will never attack a populous town.'

There are reasons for believing that at the close of the Sixth Dynasty, when the land was threatened with an invasion by negroes from the south, the Government invited Nubians, known as the People of the Bow, to come in to guard the frontier or the Gate of the South. According to Petrie these Nubians, who were, he thinks, much like the modern Gallas, established a principality in Upper Egypt. The tombs of these princes he found recently at Qau.

The Egyptian sage, Ipuwer, to whose admonitions reference has already been made, uttered remarks which appear to support this view. We may cite the following: 'The door-(keepers) say "Let us go and plunder."' 'The bowman is ready. The wrong-doer is everywhere.' 'The troops which we recruited for ourselves are become a people of the Bow, and have come to destroy.'

These scanty records and the great dearth of monuments and works of art that can be referred to these centuries show us that during this time Egypt was in a state of chaos. Trade was at a standstill: 'Men do not sail north to (Byblos) to-day. What shall we do for cedars for our mummies, with the produce of which priests are buried, and with the oil of which (chiefs) are embalmed as far as Keftiu. They come no more. Gold is lacking.' 'Lacking are grain, charcoal.' Agriculture, too, was in a bad way. 'A man goes to plough with his shield.' 'Nile overflows, (yet) no one ploughs for him.' 'Grain has perished on every side.' The system of irrigation was impaired. 'Upper Egypt has become dry (wastes).' 'The desert is throughout the land.'

There are some indications that there had been a rebellion, and that the power of the nobles had been overthrown. It is possible, however, that the country had come under the rule of alien dynasties, under which the nobles would have suffered more than the peasants. This condition of things the Sage bewails. 'The washerman refuses to carry his load.' 'Poor men are become masters of good things.' 'He who could make for himself no sandals is (now) the possessor of riches.' 'The wealthy are in mourning. The poor man is full of joy. Every town says "Let us suppress the powerful among us."' 'Gold and lapis lazuli, silver and malachite, carnelian and bronze, stone of Yebhet and . . . are fastened on the necks of female slaves. Good things are in the land, (yet) mistresses of houses say, "would that we had something to eat."'

'Their (noble ladies') limbs are in sad plight by reason of (their) rags.' 'The son of a man of rank is no (longer) distinguished from him who has no such father.' 'The children of princes are dashed against the walls.' 'Those who were clad in fine linen are beaten. Noble ladies suffer like slave girls.' 'All female slaves are free with their tongues. When their mistress speaks, it is irksome to the servants.' 'Princes are hungry and in distress.' 'Serfs become lords of serfs.' 'The corn of Egypt is common property.' 'The children of princes are cast out in the streets.' 'A few lawless men have ventured to despoil the land of kingship.' 'Men have ventured to rebel against the Uraeus.' 'The possessors of robes are (now) in rags. He who never wove for himself is (now) a man of wealth.' 'The chiefs of the land flee. Noble ladies go hungry.' 'No craftsman works. The enemies of the land have spoilt its crafts.'

Whether as the result of foreign invasions or of internal revolution or both combined, the former ruling class had evidently been removed from its commanding position. Law and order were at an end, and the bulk of the people were miserable. 'The virtuous man walks in mourning,' continues the gloomy Sage, 'on account of that which has happened in the land.' 'Women are lacking and no (children) are conceived.' 'Plague

FIG. 79. Statue of Mere, a Theban Prince.

is throughout the land. Blood is everywhere. Death is not lacking.'

'Many dead are buried in the river. The stream is a sepulchre, and the place of embalmment has become stream.' 'Squalor is throughout the land.' 'The towns are destroyed.' 'Crocodiles are glutted with what they have captured. Men go to these of their own accord.' 'Elephantine and Thinis are (the dominion of) Upper Egypt, yet without paying taxes owing to civil strife.' 'Mirth has perished and is (no longer) made. It is groaning that is throughout the land.' 'Great and small (say) "I wish I might die."' 'There is no food. To-day, like what is the taste thereof to-day?' 'Lower Egypt weeps.'

Such is the picture left by Ipuwer. During the latter part, however, of the rule of the Tenth Dynasty the princes of Thebes were increasing in power as defenders of the Heracleopolite kingdom against invaders from the south. As the power of these kings diminished, that of the Theban princes increased. At length, about 2160 B.C., Intef, or Antef, the ruling prince of Thebes, proclaimed himself first king of the Eleventh Dynasty, and he and his immediate successors gradually drove out the invaders and re-established law and order throughout Egypt.

Few remains of this intermediate period have come to light as the results of excavations. Great nobles were no longer in a position to erect lofty tombs or to furnish them with luxurious fittings; it seems to have been impossible even to preserve those of an earlier age, for these were frequently plundered and allowed to fall into decay.

The chief items of evidence for this period, besides the lists of the kings, are the literary works, consisting mostly of lamentations, later copies of which have come down to us. It is true that it cannot be proved that all such works were written at this time, though some certainly date from this unsettled period. The close resemblance to these of several others suggests

that we may attribute all this 'lamentation' literature to the
years lying between the Sixth and the Eleventh Dynasties.

BOOKS

Breasted, J. H. *A History of Egypt* (New York, 1912).
The Cambridge Ancient History, vol. i (Cambridge, 1923).
Hall, H. R. *The Ancient History of the Near East* (London, 1912).

13
Chronological Summary

IN this volume we have been recounting events that took place
between 2600 and 2200 B.C. This was a stirring period in the
world's history, and the movements of nomad peoples at this
time reverberated throughout the Old World, so that their
effects were felt from the Atlantic Ocean almost to within sight
of the Pacific.

It was not altogether a new experience to the peoples of the
river-side regions to be invaded and over-run by nomads from
the steppes and deserts. During predynastic times shepherds
from Palestine had invaded the Delta, while the stone-bowl
makers of the Eastern Desert had settled higher up on the Nile.
The unification of the Egyptian kingdom under Menes had put
an end to such invasions, and the organization of the Old Kingdom had been sufficiently powerful to keep such foes at a
distance. The Sumerian cities of Mesopotamia, too, had felt the
power of such invaders, and had, from 3097 to 2961 B.C., been
under the domination of the kings of Maer.

A new power had been arising early in the third millennium;
this time on the northern steppe. Here the people of the ochre
graves, who were, we believe, descendants of late Palaeolithic
hunters, reinforced later by members of the Final Capsian
invasion of Europe, were driving their herds of cattle on the

grasslands and burying their dead under mounds or kurgans. We have found reason for believing them to have been mainly of the type now known as Nordic, and to have spoken the primitive Indo-European or Aryan tongue. Though they were for the most part nomad herdsmen, using implements of stone, some, living on the northern flank of the Caucasus mountains, had obtained implements of copper from their neighbours to the south, and used axes of a type known much earlier in Mesopotamia. Some little time before 2600 B.c. they had, according to our conjecture, tamed the horse, which added vastly to their mobility, and, if we may believe the attractive theories of Ellsworth Huntington, they were about this time suffering from scarcity of grass, due to a period of drought.

We have suggested that it was, perhaps, some of these people of the Northern Steppe who had penetrated the mountain barrier to the south, and were threatening the empire of Sargon towards the close of his reign about 2700 B. c. We have suggested that they may have been horsemen and that they were probably the peoples known later as the men of Su and Gu. Whether this be so or not, the men of Gu, known now as Gutium, attacked Shargali-shari in 2622 B. c. It seems likely that they had appeared in Northern Mesopotamia before the latter date, and had caused unrest among the nomad or quasi-nomad peoples of Southwest Asia, for in 2626 B.c. there was trouble in Palestine, and the people of that part had threatened Egypt so seriously as to necessitate a punitive expedition and the destruction of their villages. From this time on there was constant trouble on the borders of Egypt, though the monarchy was powerful enough to keep the raiders at a distance. Trouble also occurred on the confines of Mesopotamia, where the descendants of Sargon with difficulty kept the invaders at bay until 2541 B. c., when they broke through and destroyed for a time the Sumerian civilization.

It was about 2600 B. c., or perhaps a trifle earlier, so we believe that the men of the Northern Steppe pushed outwards in every direction. It was, perhaps, due to their raids, or it may have been to the drought that was the ultimate cause of both, that the people of Anau abandoned the village on their North Kurgan. It is to this date, or to the few centuries that follow it, that we attribute the spread of the potter's art, with the technique of painted wares, to Sind and the Punjab in India and to various places in China, the most easterly of which is almost within sight of the Pacific Ocean.

It is about the same date that we attribute the destruction of Cucuteni and Erösd and the other villages of the Black Earth lands, which seems certainly to be due to these nomads, and to a whole series of movements of peoples throughout much of the south-east corner of Europe.

Some of the people of the Black Earth lands fled southwards to Thessaly, or were carried thither by their conquerors. They settled in the east of that country in strongly fortified villages, such as that at Dhimini. Here they introduced the cultivation of bread wheat and painted pottery, very like that used on the Black Earth lands; this in Thessaly is called Dhimini ware.

The great mass of the nomad steppe-men seem to have passed into the Middle Danube basin and settled on the plain of Hungary. Here they seem to have made themselves masters of the Danubian peasants, though some of the latter moved northwards through the Moravian gap, westwards up the Danube to Münchshofen and southwards up the valley of the Morava and down that of the Vardar into the western part of Thessaly.

About the same time some people, probably from some part of Asia Minor, settled on the deserted mound of Hissarlik, which they defended with stout walls, perhaps for fear of attacks by the steppe-men. This settlement is known as the Second City or more briefly as Hissarlik II. About the same time some traders, perhaps from the Cyclades or possibly from some port on the coast of Asia Minor, visited the mouth of the Don and carried many elements of Cycladic culture to the dwellers by the banks of the Don and the Donetz. Other Cycladic traders had already at an earlier date settled on the north-east coast of Crete and on the island of Mochlos, where they erected tombs, in some ways resembling those on the Cycladic islands, but showing the idea of an ossuary like the beehive tombs of the Mesara plain in the south of Crete.

We must now follow the fortunes of the Danubian peasants who had fled through the Moravian gap. Some of these turned to the east into Galicia, and seemed to have mixed there with epipalaeolithic folk and refugees from the Black Earth settlement of Horodnica. Others turned westward into Silesia and settled in the neighbourhood of Nosswitz. From Bohemia some peasants passed down the Elbe to the neighbourhood of Magdeburg, where they were joined later by others who had left Bohemia a generation or two later; it was at this latter time, about 2500 B.C., that others settled in the neighbourhood of Rössen. Others again moved higher up the Danube valley.

During the greater part of the next century, until 2416 B.C., the men of Gutium ruled all the cities of Mesopotamia and the records are silent. Only of Lagash and Umma have we any information. At the former city Gudea kept alive the old Sumerian civilization, while it was a *patesi* of the latter, Utukhegal, who expelled the men of Gutium and founded the Fifth Dynasty of Erech, which gave way in 2409 B.C. to the Third Dynasty of Ur.

During the long reign of Pepi II the defence of Egypt became weaker, and the hill-tribes from Judaea were threatening the frontier, and at his death, about 2478 B.C., the country was scarcely able to keep out the invaders. At last, in 2475 B.C., the Sixth Dynasty was brought to an end by the simultaneous invasion of the land by the hill-tribes of the north-west and the

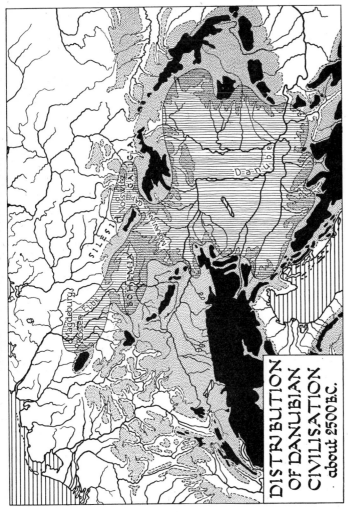

DISTRIBUTION OF DANUBIAN CIVILISATION about 2500 B.C.

Magdeburg
Rössen
Silesia
Grossgartach
Bohemia
Würzburg
Galicia
Danube

Fig. 80.

Nubians, assisted by negroes, from the south. Then followed the period of chaos, known usually as the First Intermediate period, so graphically described by Ipuwer, the gloomy sage.

About 2500 B.C. the Danubian peasants who had settled in Western Thessaly moved southwards until they reached the Gulf of Corinth, while a little later some seem to have got as far south as Tiryns. A generation later some of the Dhimini folk from East Thessaly followed the same course, so that in the villages around Corinth we find evidence of the presence of both these recent invaders of Thessaly, as well as of some of the earlier Thessalians, who had reached the Gulf some centuries before. Several centuries earlier, about 2800 B.C., some of the Cycladic traders had landed on the coast of Argolis and made settlements at Nauplia, Tiryns, and Mycenae; by 2400 B.C., or soon after, they had reached the Gulf of Corinth, where they settled in the villages founded by the earlier arrivals. Some people think that the names Corinth and Tiryns, and other names ending in -inth, were given to these and other places by these Cycladic traders, who seem to have come in the first instance from Caria.

The Danubian peasants still worked for their own new lords within the Carpathian ring, and those who had passed to the north and west moved still farther afield. They spread farther in Silesia, to Ottitz and Jordansmühl, where they were joined by fresh emigrants from Bohemia. The Magdeburg peasants crossed the mountains and passed down the Neckar valley to the Rhine and settled at Hinkelstein near Worms; here they were followed at a short interval by the steppe-men. Some of those who had passed up the Danube descended the Neckar and settled at Flomborn near Mainz, and between 2400 and 2300 B.C. these had joined forces with the men of Hinkelstein to form new settlements near Plaidt in the Eifel mountains. Some of the Rössen folk had crossed the Thuringian mountains and, passing down the valley of the Sieg, reached the Rhine near Bonn, while

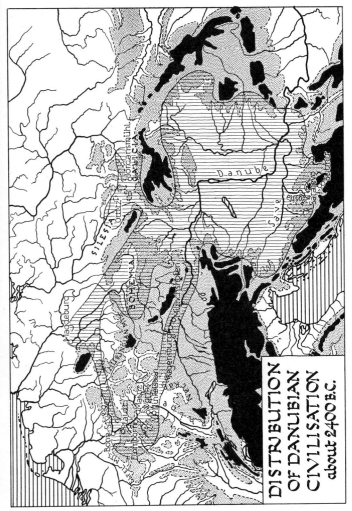

DISTRIBUTION OF DANUBIAN CIVILISATION about 2400 B.C.

Fig. 81.

others travelled up the Danube to Münchshofen near Regensburg, where they were joined soon afterwards by others that had
left the Hungarian plain at a later date. Lastly, some peasants,
who had already come into contact with the invaders, passed up
the Save valley, and up that of the Bosna, to Butmir near Sarajevo.

During the rule of the Third Dynasty of Ur, which arose
in 2409 B.C., Sumerian civilization revived, especially under
Dungi. This Dynasty lasted until 2311 B.C., when it was destroyed by the Elamites. Most of the Sumerian cities, however,
retained their independence, though under the leadership of
the kings of Isin, for more than a century. Chaos still reigned
in Egypt, though some semblance of order was re-established at
Heracleopolis, where two successive Dynasties of kings attempted
to govern the land. Conditions were better at Thebes, where
princes, probably of Nubian extraction, were defending the
country from southern invaders.

During this century the mixed population that had settled
at the head of the Gulf in the neighbourhood of Corinth set
out to explore the unknown lands of the west. In the first
instance they made settlements in the island of Leukas, which
lies at the mouth of the gulf in the Adriatic; then, starting from
that base, they crossed the sea to the Italian coast, where traces
of their handiwork have been found at Matera and Molfetta.
It seems likely that before 2300 B.C. they had reached Megara
Hyblaea and other sites in the south-eastern corner of Sicily.

There was a still further spread of the Danubian peasants at
this time. Some of those who had settled at Plaidt and elsewhere in the Eifel mountains seem to have descended the valley
of the Rhine towards Cologne and crossed thence to the Meuse
near Liége. Here they made settlements, and before the close
of the century had advanced to the neighbourhood of Brussels.
Others, either from the neighbourhood of Flomborn or of
Hinkelstein, or perhaps from some other settlement still higher

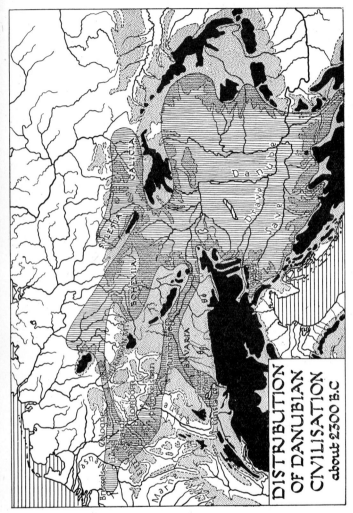

DISTRIBUTION OF DANUBIAN CIVILISATION about 2300 B.C

Fig. 82.

up the river, seem to have gone westwards, and ultimately to have reached the valley of the Marne, and to have passed down that valley to that of the Seine near Paris.

From the neighbourhood of Münchshofen in Bavaria some of the Danubian peasants moved southwards to Aichbühl on the Federsee moor, where they took to erecting their dwellings upon piles, and before the close of the century some of these peasants had reached Lake Constance. It is possible that here they met some of the epipalaeolithic descendants of the Maglemose people, who had at an earlier date ascended the Rhine from the coasts of the North Sea. Other folk from the Federsee moor established themselves around the lakes to the east, while by about 2300 B.C. some had reached Laibach moor.

Towards the beginning of this century, about 2400 B.C., the walls of the Second City of Hissarlik were rebuilt, and a more active trade was prosecuted in several directions, both by sea and by land. By sea the products of Hissarlik reached the island of Euboea and the coasts of the Adriatic and of Sicily. The main overland trade was up the Danube valley and through the Moravian gap; also into Bohemia and thence into Saxony.

The little kingdom of Isin, with the small group of cities that it governed, retained its independence after the fall of Ur in 2301 B.C., and here a number of kings ruled and kept alive the Sumerian civilization. The Amurru were always threatening this little kingdom, and at length in 2169 B.C. they broke through the defences that had been erected near Sippar to keep them back, and Sumu-abu their leader fixed his capital at Babylon, where he founded the First Babylonian Dynasty. In Egypt matters continued much as before, but after 2200 B.C. the kings of Heracleopolis became more and more dependent upon the princes of Thebes, until, about 2160 B.C. Antef, one of these, assumed the sovereignty and established himself as the first king of the Eleventh Dynasty.

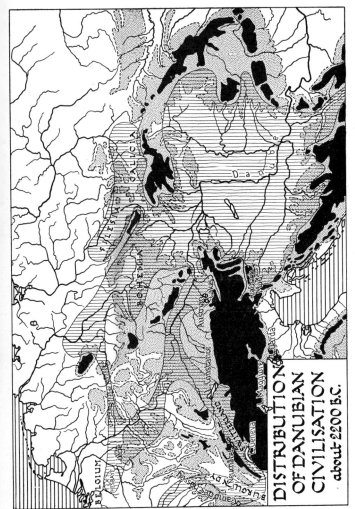

DISTRIBUTION OF DANUBIAN CIVILISATION about 2200 B.C.

Fig. 83.

The peasants from the Danube basin continued to establish villages in La Hesbaye in Belgium, but their farther advance was hindered by stretches of light soil, covered in places with dunes and drifting sand, which were unsuitable for cultivation. The lake-dwellers who had settled by the shores of Lake Constance pushed on to Lake Neuchâtel and to many other of the lakes of North-east Switzerland. Here they seem to have mixed with epipalaeolithic folk, who still retained some elements of Azilian culture. By 2200 B.C. they had made many settlements around the Lake of Geneva, while later they seem to have pushed westwards into Burgundy, where they settled on the hill-top of the Camp de Chassey in the department of Saône-et-Loire. Some of the lake-dwellers by the shores of the Austrian lakes seem to have crossed the Brenner Pass during this century and settled at the southern end of Lago di Garda. Not long after 2200 B.C. some of these had reached the marshes at the southern end of Lago Maggiore.

Those who had been engaged in maritime activities, and in carrying Aegean products from the Gulf of Corinth to Italy and Sicily, appear to have extended their trade about this time. They were in touch with Sardinia and the Balearic islands, and, using the south-eastern corner of Sicily as a base, they carried their ventures as far as the Ligurian coast, the South of France, Spain, and even Portugal. How early they reached the Atlantic is not quite clear, but it must have been before 2200 B.C.

The trade between the City of Hissarlik II and the western lands continued, and a knobbed ivory object, dating from the third phase of the City, has been described from Nora in Portugal. The most active trade from Hissarlik was, however, with the Danube basin. The traders, carrying Asiatic wares, seem to have travelled up the Danube to the neighbourhood of Vienna, or even farther. Some seem to have passed through the Moravian gap, while others entered Bohemia and explored the mineral resources of the Erzgebirge, where they found deposits, not only of copper, but of tin.

Thus the irruption of the steppe-folk, while it brought to an end for a time the civilization of Egypt, and nearly destroyed the Sumerian civilization in Mesopotamia, had far-reaching effects in Europe. The pressure of the Northern steppe-folk drove the peasants from the Danube basin to move farther and faster than before, so that by 2200 B.C. they had reached Belgium near Liége, and had perhaps entered the Seine basin. At the same time they had spread to Bosnia and to some of the Italian lakes. Thus the practice of grain-growing, of keeping domesticated animals, and of the potter's art, spread over a large part of the continent of Europe, though the knowledge of metallurgy lagged behind.

In the meantime the commercial cities of Asia Minor, of which Hissarlik was the most important, were carrying on a trade with the Danube basin and Bohemia, with many of the Aegean islands, and with the coasts of the Adriatic. Some of the Cycladic traders, who had for long dominated the Aegean, were now settled at the head of the Gulf of Corinth, whence they traded with the coast of Italy and the south-east corner of Sicily. From the latter centre they, or people influenced by their culture, carried civilization to the European coasts of the Western Mediterranean, and through the Strait of Gibraltar to the coast of Portugal.

Thus both by land and by sea civilization was spreading over almost all the continent of Europe. The advance guard of the peasants had lost the art of metallurgy and were dependent on stone for their tools. How far the mariners were influenced at the outset by the search for metal is not clear, but eventually a knowledge of metal did spread along the coasts. How the two streams met in North-west Europe must be left to be described in our next volume.

INDEX

Abi-sare, 136, 137.
Agade, 38–40, 86, 88, 128, 129, 135, 157.
Agio Andreas, 52.
Aichbühl, 69, 71, 154.
Ambracian Gulf, 123, 125.
Amorgos, 85, 114, 123.
Anau, 20, 21, 40, 41, 90, 147.
Andersson, J. G., 41.
Anghelu Ruju, 121.
Annecy, Lake, 69, 81.
Anshan, 131, 135, 136.
Antef, 144, 154.
Antiparos, 114.
Arad, 96.
Arbela, 129, 135.
Arena Candida, 112, 123.
Arkalochori, 104.
Arne, T. J., 44.
Arrapkha, 129.
Atkinson, T. D., 84.
Attersee, 69, 80, 81.
Auvernier, 74, 77.

Babylon, 135–7, 154, 157.
Bashimi, 136.
Bates, Oric, 116.
Berg, Dr., 17.
Bombah, Gulf of, 116.
Boroffka, G., 28.
Bourget, Lake, 69, 81.
Breasted, J. H., 140, 145.
Brooks, C. E. P., 98.
Burkitt, M. C., 80.
Bur-Sin, 133, 136, 137.
Butmir, 63–7, 112, 123, 124, 151, 152.
Byblos, 141.

Caberg, 68.
Camp de Chassey, Le, 80, 155, 156.
Carchemish, 31.
Cephissus, 56–8.
Chaeronea, 56, 57.
Chalcis, 123–5.
Chatzedakis, Dr., 104.
Chen-fan, 42, 43.
Chernigov, 27.
Chih Kai Chai, 42.
Chin Hsi, 43.
Ching Wang Chai, 42.
Chirospilia, 126.
Constance, Lake, 71, 76, 79, 81, 153–6.
Corinth, 56–8, 118–26, 150–8.
Cortaillod, 74.
Csorvas, 96.
Cucuteni, 44, 46, 52, 53, 55, 67, 147.
Cyrus, 19.

Darius, 19.
Dhimini, 52–8, 74, 93, 94, 123–7, 147, 150.
Doughty, C. M., 10, 19.
Drakhmani, 56, 57.

Droop, J. P., 109.
Dubrum, 129.
Dungi, 88, 131–3, 136, 137, 152.

Ebert, M., 21, 25.
Egelsee, 75.
E-irridupizir, 129.
Elam, 131–3, 135, 136, 152.
Elephantine, 144.
Enridapizir, 129.
Erech, 128, 130, 135, 148, 157.
Erösd, 44, 46, 52, 53, 55, 67, 74, 93, 147.
Evans, Sir Arthur, 88, 90, 99, 100, 109, 116.

Fars, 8.
Fatyanovo, 48, 49.
Federsee, 71, 81, 153, 154.
Fellenberg, Dr. von, 72.
Feng-tien, 43.
Flomborn, 62, 63, 67, 68, 150–3.
Font, 74, 76.
Frankfort, H., 58, 83, 124, 125, 127.

Galu-Babbar, 130.
Garda, Lago di, 69, 80, 81, 155, 156.
Geneva, Lake of, 80, 81, 155, 156.
Giles, P., 34.
Gimil-dural, 128.
Gimil-Sin, 133, 137.
Glotz, G., 109.
Gonia, 123, 126, 127.
Gournia, 100, 101.
Grand Pressigny, Le, 80, 81.
Gravis, A., 68.
Greng, 77.
Grotta San Lazzaro, 118.
Grotte-des-Fées, 121, 122.
Gu, 39, 40, 128, 136, 146.
Gudea, 130–2, 148.
Guévaux, 77.
Gungunum, 136, 137.
Guthrie, Dr. Douglas, 76.
Gutium, 128–30, 136, 137, 146, 148, 157.

Hagia Marina, 55–7.
Hall, H. R., 41, 145.
Halle, 61, 67.
Halys, 87, 88, 132–5.
Hal Saflieni, 120, 121.
Hammurabi, 40.
Harappa, 41.
Hatti, 138.
Hemp, W., 121.
Heracleopolis, 140, 152, 154.
Hieraconpolis, 116.
Hierapetra, 100, 101.
Hinkelstein, 60, 62, 67, 150–3.
Hirth, Dr., 43.
Hissarlik, 25, 32, 46, 50, 90–118, 123–7, 147–58.
Horodnica, 60, 67, 148.

Index

159

Horus, 139.
Hrozný, F., 36, 88.
Huc, E. R., 18, 19.
Huntington, Ellsworth, 8, 16–19, 50, 51, 98, 146.

Ibi-Sin, 132, 133, 137.
Igesaus, 137.
Indre-et-Loire, 80.
Intef, 144.
Ipuwer, 141, 144, 150.
Ishtar, 129.
Isin, 135–7, 152, 154, 157.

Jackowice, 26, 27, 32.
Jeneffe, 67, 68.
Jordansmühl, 47, 65, 67, 150, 151.

Kaphtor, 88.
Kara Euyuk, 36, 87, 132, 135, 138.
Keftiu, 141.
Keller, F., 78, 80.
Kerkuk, 129, 135.
Khakhu, 130.
Khalandriani, 52, 85.
Khalepji, 44.
Kherson, 26, 49.
Kiev, 26, 32, 44, 49.
King, L. W., 138.
Kish, 37, 40, 97.
Knossos, 99, 100, 109, 115, 123.
Konstantinovka, 32.
Korakou, 56, 57, 123, 126.
Kossinna, G., 28, 35.
Kuban, 22–4, 26–8, 33, 37, 38, 51, 86, 88, 90.
Ku-ki, 88.

La Hesbaye, 66–8, 155, 156.
Lagash, 129, 130, 135, 136, 148.
Laibach, 69, 80, 81, 154, 155.
Langdon, S., 40, 132.
Larsa, 135–7.
Lasirab, 129.
Latham, Dr., 34.
Lattrigen, 76.
Leaf, W., 99.
Lengyel, 47.
Leukas or Levkas, 117–27, 152.
Liége, 66–8, 152, 153, 158.
Locraz or Lüscherz, 70.
Lugal-annatum, 130.

MacIver, D. Randall, 116.
Maer, 135, 145.
Magda, 130.
Magdeburg, 60, 67, 148–51.
Maggiore, Lago, 69, 80, 81, 155, 156.
Maglemose, 28, 30, 72, 79, 154.
Maikop, 23–5, 28, 30, 31, 38.
Malta, 110, 120, 121, 123, 127.
Markhashi, 132.
Marshall, Sir John, 41, 42.
Martin, Henri, 81.
Mas d'Azil, 71.
Matera, 123, 125, 127, 152.
Matrenza, 123, 127.

Megara Hyblaea, 123, 127, 152.
Meilen, 78, 79.
Melos, 52, 56, 82, 84–6, 95, 114, 123.
Melukhkha, 130.
Memphis, 140.
Menes, 145.
Mere, 143.
Merikara, 139, 140.
Merseburg, 61, 67.
Mesara plain, 100, 105–12, 115, 116, 120, 123, 148.
Mien Chih Hsien, 42, 43.
Migir-Sin, 133.
Minns, Ellis H., 38.
Mirabella, Bay of, 100, 101.
Mochlos, 31, 100, 110, 112, 115, 116, 120, 123, 148.
Mohenjodaro, 41, 42.
Molfetta, 123, 127, 152.
Mondsee, 69, 80, 81.
Monte Racello, 119, 123.
Moosseedorf, 70, 73, 76, 77.
Moret, A., 140.
Morges, 70.
Mosso, A., 99, 104.
Münchshofen, 62–7, 71, 79, 81, 151–4.
Munro, R. 80.
Mycenae, 56, 58, 115, 116, 123, 150.
Myres, J. L., 16, 94, 98.

Nal, 41.
Nammakhni, 129, 130.
Naucratis, 130.
Naxos, 83, 114, 123.
Nejd, 10, 13.
Neuchâtel, Lake of, 70–81, 155, 156.
Niederwyl, Lake, 75.
Ningandu, 129.
Nippur, 129, 135.
Nosswitz, 60, 67, 148, 149.
Novocherkask, 32.
Novogrigoryevka, 31.

Ober-Siggingen, 77.
Ofnet, 72, 79.
Omal, 66–8.
Orchomenos, 56–9.
Ottitz, 65, 150, 151.
Oul, 22.

Palaikastro, 101.
Paros, 32, 82, 114, 123.
Peet, T. Eric, 110, 127.
Pelos, 114.
Pepi II, 139, 140, 148.
Percival, J., 68.
Petrie, Sir Flinders, 140.
Phaestos, 99, 100.
Phylakopi, 52, 84, 85.
Plaidt, 62, 67, 150–3.
Plataea, 116.
Platanus, 105.
Port-Conty, 71, 74.
Pu Chao Chai, 42.
Pumpelly, R., 40.
Puydt, M. de, 68.

Qau, 141.

Reinerth, H., 71, 77.
Rhodes, 91.
Richensee, 77.
Richtofen, F. von, 43.
Rimash, 130.
Robenhausen, 74.
Rössen, 61, 67, 149, 150.
Rostovtzeff, M., 19, 25, 36, 38.
Rügen, 72.

Saint-Aubin, 74.
Sarajevo, 63, 67, 151, 152.
Sargon, 38, 40, 86, 88, 128, 131, 132, 146.
Schaffhausen, 72, 81.
Schafis, 76.
Schenk, A., 78.
Schliemann, H., 97, 99.
Schmidt, R. R., 71, 76.
Schötz, 77.
Schussenried, 69, 81.
Seager, R. B., 101, 104, 106, 107, 109.
Seal Island, 116.
Seistan, 13, 19, 41.
Sema Ts'ien, 43.
Sesklo, 52, 54–6.
Sha Kuo T'un, 43.
Shargali-shari, 146.
Shen Nung, 44.
Shu-Sin, 133.
Sind, 41, 147.
Si-ning, 42, 43.
Siphnos, 52, 56, 114, 123.
Sippar, 129, 133, 135, 136, 154.
Spercheios, 125.
Spitsyn, Dr., 26.
Steckborn, 77.
Stein, Sir Aurel, 17, 41.
Stentinello, 123, 127.
Stollhoff, Dr., 31.
Sua-ki, Subir, Su-ki, Su, 39.
Sub-artu, 39, 40.
Sumu-abu, 136, 154.
Sutz, 74, 76.
Syros, 52, 56, 85, 114, 116, 123.

Tallgren, A. M., 25, 31, 35.
Telloh, 130.

Thompson, M. S., 59.
Thrace, 55, 56, 97, 98.
Thurberg-Weinfelden, 77.
Tidanu or Tidnu, 130, 133, 135.
Tiriga(n), Tirikhan, or Tiriqan, 129, 137.
Tiryns, 56, 57, 58, 150.
Tripolje, 44.
Tsangli, 56.
Tschumi, Dr., 77.
Tsountas, Ch., 53–5.
Tzarevskaya, 24, 30, 31.

Ulski, 27, 29.
Umma, 129, 130, 135, 148.
Ur, 30, 88, 94, 116, 130–8, 148–57.
Ur-Bau, 129, 130.
Ur-Engur, 130, 133.
Urgar, 129.
Ur-id, 130.
Ur-Lammu, 131.
Ur-Lugal-banda, 132.
Ur-Nammu, 130, 137.
Ur-Nigingar, 133.
Ur-Ningirsu, 130.
Ur-Ninurta, 136, 137.
Ur-Ninsum, 129.
Usatov, 44.
Utukhegal, 129, 130, 137.

Vasiliki, 101, 102.
Villafrati, 118, 123.
Vinča, 46, 95.
Vinelz, 76, 77.
Vouga, P., 70, 74, 76, 77, 78, 80.
Vrokastro, 31.

Wace, A. J. B., 59.
Wangen, 74.
Wauwil, 70, 76, 77, 78.
Wei Tartars, 16, 17.
Wilkins, A., 116.
Woolley, C. L., 116.

Xanthoudides, S., 109.

Yang Shao Tsun, 42.
Yao, 43, 44.
Yin Hsien, 42, 43.
Yortan, 112, 123.

PRINTED IN ENGLAND AT THE UNIVERSITY PRESS OXFORD
BY JOHN JOHNSON PRINTER TO THE UNIVERSITY